Materials Science
PLASTICS

making use of the secrets of matter

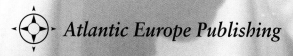
Atlantic Europe Publishing

First published in 2003 by
Atlantic Europe Publishing Company Ltd.

Reprinted in 2005

Author
Brian Knapp, BSc, PhD

Art Director
Duncan McCrae, BSc

Senior Designer
Adele Humphries, BA, PGCE

Editors
Mary Sanders, BSc, and Gillian Gatehouse

Illustrations
David Woodroffe

Design and production
EARTHSCAPE EDITIONS

Scanning and retouching
Global Graphics sro, Czech Republic

Print
WKT Company Ltd., China

Materials Science – **Volume 1: Plastics**
A CIP record for this book is available from the British Library

ISBN 1 86214 315 3

Acknowledgments
The publishers would like to thank the following for their kind help and advice: *Jack Brettle*; *Janet Brettle*; *Duncan Cooper*; *Graham Gatehouse*; *David M. Graham and Robert A. (Robin) Graham*; *Guthrie Plantation & Agricultural Sdn Bhd and the Kampulan Guthrie Estate*; *Michael Hoare*; *Peter Limieux of Athabasca Glacier Icewalks*; *Pippa McCrae*; *Paul Millett*; *Peter and Ellie Nalle*; *Royal Berkshire Fire and Rescue Service*; *Pete Thompson*.

Picture credits
All photographs are from the Earthscape Editions photolibrary except the following: (c=center t=top b=bottom l=left r=right)
Fire Research Station 14b; ICI 17t, 17b.

This product is manufactured from sustainable managed forests. For every tree cut down, at least one more is planted.

Contents

1: The nature of plastics   4

What science calls plastic   4
What is a polymer?   6
Plastics vs. fibers   7
What polymers are made of   7
Natural polymers   8
Thermosets and thermoplastics   11
Range of plastics   12
Plastics, electricity, and heat   13
Plastics and fire   14
Plastics and chemicals   15
Plastics, weight, and strength   15
Adding to polymers   15
How plastics are made   17
How plastics are joined   22
Decorative laminates   22
Reinforcing a plastic   22
Recycling a plastic   23
Resin Identification Code   26

2: Common plastics   27

The main types of polymers used   27
Simple plastics   28
Acrylic plastics   39
Diene plastics   42
Complex plastics   43
Polyesters   50
Polyester paints and resins   53

Set glossary   58

Set index   65

(*Left*) A "blister" pack of tablets seen from the back. The plastic on the back is easily compressed to allow the tablets to be pushed out of the pack.

1: The nature of plastics

Everyone thinks they know what plastic is because it is all around us in plastic bags, plastic window frames, plastic keys on computers, and so on. The list is seemingly endless.

Actually, we simply call all of these objects "plastic" without thinking about whether or not plastic is one material or many. In fact, the simple word "plastic" is used to cover a list of materials that is almost as endless as the uses to which plastics are put.

The word "PLASTIC" takes its meaning from the French, Greek, and Latin, and can broadly be defined as "having the characteristic of being moldable." Indeed, one meaning of the word "plastic" is something that can be molded into a new shape either by heat or pressure. However, since the first moldable material was invented, an enormous range of materials has been made using CARBON COMPOUNDS. They are plastic materials, usually just called plastics. They can all be molded or shaped as a result of the use of heat or pressure.

Most materials that we will consider in this book have the capacity to be molded, that is, they have the property called PLASTICITY. At the same time, they have a wide range of other properties such as low DENSITY, low electrical CONDUCTIVITY, transparency, and toughness.

What science calls plastic

Just as there are many types of metal (aluminum, iron, copper, and so on), there are many kinds of plastics (polyethylene, styrofoam, and so on), although they often have less familiar names. Indeed, there are more kinds of plastics than any other kind of material. Thus the material used for soft drink bottles is not at all the same as the material used for holding hot drinks or the material

(*Right and below*) Plastics are everywhere. And they are usually cheap, too. That is why you are just as likely to find plastics in the kitchens of the developed world (for example, this percolator) as in the developing world (for example, in these colorful bowls and buckets). In many cases they do the same job as metal items, but often more cheaply.

used for making computer cases, even though they are all made of "plastic."

In this book you will find out just how various these materials are, what properties they have, and how people can design new plastic materials.

What is a polymer?

Before we begin our study of plastics, there are two words that will come up time and time again. It is important, at the outset, to be clear about their meaning. They are POLYMER and RESIN (see page 11).

Because the word "plastic" has many meanings in everyday life, scientists need to use more precise terms like "polymer." A polymer is a substance consisting of many identical building blocks. To a scientist all the materials we call plastics are polymers because that is how they are formed—of identical parts linked together to form giant MOLECULES. Some examples are threads, such as silk, others are liquids, such as shellac, and yet others are found as blocks or sheets, such as rubber.

(*Left*) A fishing lure made of natural rubber.

(*Below*) This is a molecule of natural rubber. It is a polymer. The long polymer chains are made up of repeating units of isoprene. Synthetic rubber can be made artificially using isoprene derived from crude oil. For more on how synthetic polymers such as this can be made, see page 11.

Hydrogen

Carbon

CH$_3$ group

(*Above*) These door stops are made from natural rubber. Over many years they have rotted due to the effects of heat, moisture, and light. Synthetic versions of rubber can be enhanced to make them more resistant to weathering. This is both the advantage and the disadvantage of synthetic polymers over natural ones—natural polymers degrade naturally and therefore do not last very long; synthetic polymers degrade hardly at all— which is fine until we want to get rid of them.

See **Vol. 7: Fibers** *for more on synthetic fibers.*

See **Vol. 2: Metals** *for more on steel.*

All of the substances just mentioned are naturally occurring giant linked molecules called polymers.

By the 19th century an understanding of molecules allowed scientists to make new polymers—or SYNTHETICS as they are called. Celluloid (see page 46) is one of the earliest examples.

Plastics vs. fibers

Many plastics and synthetic fibers are made from the same polymers. However, while fibers are spun into threads in which all the molecules are lined up in long chains, plastics are linked in three dimensions to make solid objects, sheets, or films.

What polymers are made of

The idea of substances made of long chains is the key to understanding plastics. These chains can be far longer than any other substance. The size of the chain and the way it links to other chains are the key to the different properties of all plastics.

To understand why this is so important, think of the difference between steel and a plastic. Steel is made of iron atoms with a few carbon atoms scattered among them. There are no chains in this material, so steel cannot be turned into other materials.

A plastic is made of carbon atoms linked together in a chain and often cross-linked to make a sheet. Depending on how the chain is linked, and which other atoms are in the chain, the chain can be fashioned in a multitude of ways. That is why so many different types of plastic can be created. It is also the reason many plastics can be molded and shaped.

Natural polymers

In this book we will be dealing with plastics that are produced from chemical reactions that are very precise and highly controlled. But not all of the polymer industry is like this. In fact, many natural polymers have been used for hundreds of years and continue to be used successfully today.

One of the most important is the sap from the rubber tree. Natural rubber is a polymer of isoprene (polyisoprene) and occurs in over 200 species of plant. The only important source is the tropical rubber tree (*Hevea braziliensis*), which exudes a milky fluid we call latex. The latex contains about 35% rubber.

Producing rubber is, in general, quite a low-tech process done by people who work among the rubber plantations in the developing world.

They slit the rubber tree bark and let the sap run free. It can then be collected in small cups and later be gathered into larger amounts before being transported to factories large and small.

Rubber has to be extracted from the latex using special chemicals that turn it into a solid, although it can be liquefied again for easier use. Rubber can be used to make everything from surgical gloves to face masks, from tires to rubber bands. The original chewing gum was made from chicle, the latex from another tree found in Central America.

The reason that rubber is relatively not as important a product as it once was is that there is little control over its chemical makeup, and it cannot be made in the quantities of elastic materials that are now required. Also, rubber is now just one of the thousands of products that people use both at home and in offices and factories.

A rubber tapper cuts another strip of bark at dawn (*left*). The sap immediately flows and is collected (*center*). The sap is taken to a central point and dried before being sent on for manufacture (*right*).

(*Right*) Using liquefied rubber to make surgical gloves. In this process ceramic molds in the shape of hands are carried along a conveyor belt and dipped into a bath of rubber. (*Below left*) The rubber-covered molds then go into an oven for curing, and the rubber is pulled off the formers. (*Below right*) The gloves are then blown up using compressed air to test for defects—an important stage since these gloves will be used for surgery.

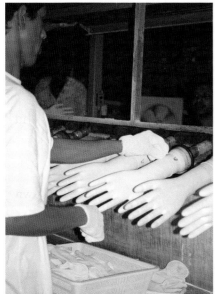

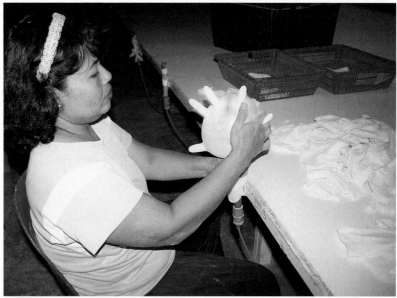

(*Left and above*) Natural rubber masks on sale and rubber gloves used for cleaning up.

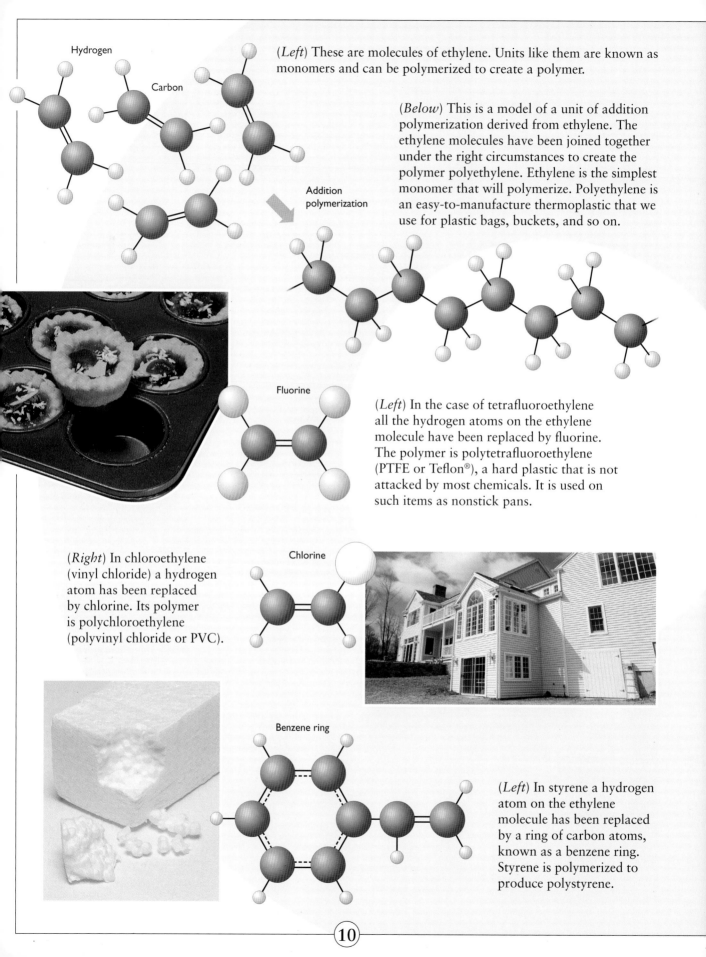

Hydrogen

Carbon

(*Left*) These are molecules of ethylene. Units like them are known as monomers and can be polymerized to create a polymer.

(*Below*) This is a model of a unit of addition polymerization derived from ethylene. The ethylene molecules have been joined together under the right circumstances to create the polymer polyethylene. Ethylene is the simplest monomer that will polymerize. Polyethylene is an easy-to-manufacture thermoplastic that we use for plastic bags, buckets, and so on.

Addition polymerization

Fluorine

(*Left*) In the case of tetrafluoroethylene all the hydrogen atoms on the ethylene molecule have been replaced by fluorine. The polymer is polytetrafluoroethylene (PTFE or Teflon®), a hard plastic that is not attacked by most chemicals. It is used on such items as nonstick pans.

(*Right*) In chloroethylene (vinyl chloride) a hydrogen atom has been replaced by chlorine. Its polymer is polychloroethylene (polyvinyl chloride or PVC).

Chlorine

Benzene ring

(*Left*) In styrene a hydrogen atom on the ethylene molecule has been replaced by a ring of carbon atoms, known as a benzene ring. Styrene is polymerized to produce polystyrene.

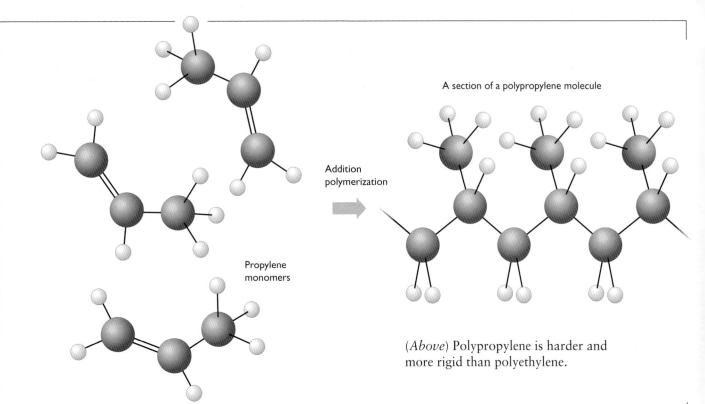

A section of a polypropylene molecule

Addition polymerization

Propylene monomers

(*Above*) Polypropylene is harder and more rigid than polyethylene.

(*Above*) Polyethylene bags containing rolls of polyethylene sheet. Both are thermoplastics.

Thermosets and thermoplastics

The other important word to remember in studying plastics is RESIN. A resin is any sticky liquid that is made from a natural living or once-living substance that, when hardened, will not dissolve in water.

The term "resin" is very broad. Varnishes and lacquers are resins. But plastics, too, are made from resins. In fact, plastics are the majority of materials made from resins.

There are two distinct types of resins: those that will get soft and can be molded when warmed time after time; and those that get soft once on heating and subsequently harden and can never be molded again. Those that can be repeatedly warmed are called thermoplastic resins (THERMOPLASTICS), and those that set hard are called thermosetting resins or THERMOSETS.

Very simple chains can easily be separated, so simple plastics tend to be thermoplastic. More complicated plastics containing different atoms tend to interlock and cannot come undone when they are heated. As a result, they tend to be thermosetting.

When a thermoset is heated, it cannot change shape but instead just gets hotter and hotter until, finally, it burns.

When a thermoplastic gets warm enough, the chains move apart, and the material becomes rubbery. To make this easier to understand, the way a plastic changes can be compared to glass. When you heat glass, it softens and then begins to get rubbery. Glass does not melt at this time; it only melts at a much higher temperature.

Some plastics do not have to be hot or even warm to the touch to be rubbery. Cling wrap and other materials will even stay rubbery in a freezer.

Range of plastics

Whether a material is used or not depends on how easy it is to work with, how easy it is to shape, how cheap it is, whether it is safe or poisonous, whether it can be made to look attractive, and so on.

In the case of plastics each property can be adjusted to help meet a need, although this is less easy to do with many other materials such as glass, metals, or natural rubber. That is why plastics are used so extensively.

Many plastics melt at relatively low temperatures and so are easy to mold. Additionally, their makeups are relatively easy to change to produce a wide variety of qualities such as color, texture, hardness, brittleness, and so on. On the downside, the raw materials, principally petroleum products, are relatively expensive, which limits the extent of their use. Because they are made from PETROCHEMICALS, the widespread use of plastics also raises concerns about their recycling.

(*Above*) These plastic optic fiber casings need to be tough but flexible, heat resistant, and even resistant to burrowing animals.

See **Vol. 5: Glass** *for more on heating glass*

(*Below*) Plastics often make it possible to add design to functionality. Plastics can be molded to shape, given translucent colors, made semitransparent, and still resist blows and fire. This is a computer casing.

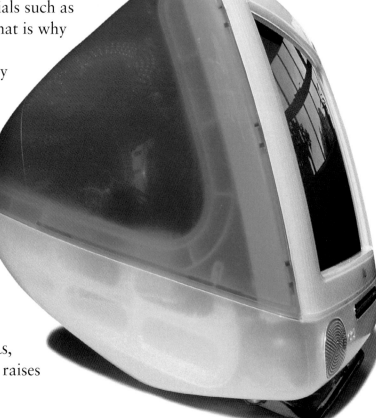

The most commonly manufactured plastics are those that can be used for a wide variety of purposes because the bigger the production, the cheaper the product tends to be. PVC is one of them. But most plastics have only a narrow range of applications. They are called speciality plastics. Nevertheless, some are still made in large quantities. Nylon and polyester—both used almost exclusively for making fabrics and binding materials—are examples of high-volume speciality plastics (see pages 48 and 50).

General-purpose plastics have simple structures made just with long chains of carbon. The more specialized plastics have more complicated chains containing other elements such as oxygen, nitrogen, or sulfur.

Again, the general-purpose polymers tend to be ones that can be warmed and reshaped time after time (thermoplastics), while the more specialized ones tend to harden after only one heating (thermosets).

The general-purpose plastics have found many uses for which there was no convenient previous alternative. Plastic bags are one example. They have also displaced many traditional materials because of their cheapness, durability, and weight. Plastics have mainly replaced galvanized steel for buckets, for instance.

Many continue to compete head to head with other materials. Synthetic fibers such as polyester compete with natural fibers such as wool and cotton; polycarbonate competes with glass for factory windows; synthetic rubber competes with natural rubber. What the increasing range of plastics has done is to broaden the choices a user has in finding a material that is suitable for a purpose at an economical price.

(*Above*) Exterior lights (called Luminaires) often use a plastic as a translucent material to help spread the light and reduce the glare from the bulb. This one is made from polycarbonate, a material tough enough to be almost vandal proof.

(*Below*) Plastics used for plugs have to resist burning, be electrical insulators, and resist hard blows.

Plastics, electricity, and heat

For a material to be able to conduct electricity, the particles in the material called ELECTRONS have to be able to move easily. They can do so in a metal, which is why metals are good CONDUCTORS of electricity. However, in a plastic the electrons are tightly bound to their ATOMS and so

See **Vol. 2: Metals** *for more on conduction.*

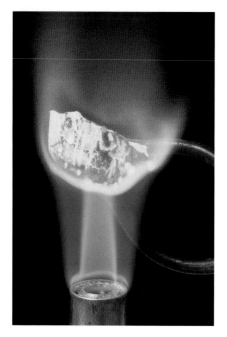

(*Above*) Some polymers are prone to give off toxic fumes and burn fiercely when heated. That is shown (*below*) in this picture of furniture covered with simple polymers. Polymers can be designed to have special properties such as resistance to heat and burning. Such properties are now mandatory for all materials used in furniture and are vital in producing protective suits, such as those used in firefighting.

cannot move even when a large electric charge is put across the material. As a result, plastics rarely conduct electricity and are therefore commonly used as electrical INSULATORS.

Similarly, most plastics are poor conductors of heat. They are therefore often used as heat insulators too. Their insulation properties can be improved further by making them into foams so that the plastic traps bubbles of air. That is the reasoning behind manufacturing foamed polystyrene—styrofoam. Styrofoam with air bubbles insulates four times better than solid polystyrene and yet is cheaper to make, takes less material, and weighs less. It is widely used for insulation between walls, as a liner to walls and ceilings, and for disposable beverage cups.

Plastics and fire

Some plastics are very flammable. Not only do these plastics burn fiercely, giving out heat that fuels the fire and can reach temperatures that even melt metal, but they also give off fumes that may be poisonous. In the past, styrofoam was used for ceiling tiles, and PVC foam was used in furnishings. During a fire they would create a dense, black toxic smoke, and the ceiling tiles would release hot drips that rapidly spread the fire. However, plastics can be made that resist catching fire, and only these specially treated materials are now used in domestic furniture.

Plastics and chemicals

Plastics can be very resistant to chemicals, and so many chemicals can be kept in plastic bottles. You can see this if you look at all of the domestic cleaning chemicals kept in a kitchen. There are soaps, bleaches, acids, and alkalis. Many are nasty substances if they get onto skin, but perfectly safe kept in a plastic bottle and if handled with plastic ("rubber") gloves.

Plastics, weight, and strength

Plastics are, in general, very lightweight materials compared to ceramics (for example, stone and tiles) and metals (for example, steel and copper). Their light weight does have advantages for many purposes, but often plastics are not as strong as metals or ceramics under pressure and so are not used in places where great stresses are involved, for example, in bridges or cranes.

(*Below*) Because rubber gloves do not react with most chemicals, they can be used to protect hands against the harmful effects of most domestic chemicals.

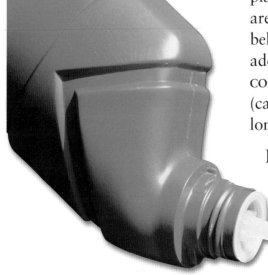

(*Below*) Cleaning chemicals can nearly all be kept in plastic containers, which are less likely to break than glass bottles.

Adding to polymers

Just as metals are given new properties and made more useful by mixing small amounts of other substances with them to make an ALLOY, plastics are given a wide range of new uses by adding small amounts of another substance to them. In the case of plastics these substances are called additives. There are special additives to change the way a plastic behaves when pulled or squashed (called PLASTICIZERS), additives that change the color of a plastic (called COLORANTS), additives that make a plastic stronger (called REINFORCERS), and additives that give a plastic a longer life (called STABILIZERS).

Plasticizers

Remember that a thermoplastic becomes more rubbery when it gets warm enough. A plasticizer is a substance that, when added, brings down the temperature at which this happens. For example, PVC without a plasticizer is normally a rigid material. In this form it is used as siding for houses or as pipes. These uses require the plastic to stay rigid even on a hot day. However, a garden hose is also made from PVC, and in this use it needs to be rubbery even below the freezing point. (If it turned rigid below the freezing point, the hose would burst if water froze inside it.) This change in property is produced by adding a plasticizer.

Colorants

Very few plastics are used in their natural colors. Unlike many other materials, many polymers cannot easily be dyed. However, even those that resist the introduction of colors can be painted.

Many plastics will mix easily with a coloring material (called a PIGMENT). This means that the plastic is colored throughout, and if it is scratched, it will keep its color. This is often much more useful than if it were painted. Black plastics (which also resist breaking down in sunlight) have carbon (soot) as a colorant. White plastics use titanium or zinc oxide.

Reinforcer

A reinforcing material is usually a completely different substance than the plastic. It may be fibers of glass (as in fiberglass, in which glass fibers are coated with plastic resin), or it may be tiny fragments of metal or even a powder of another material such as a ceramic like chalk (calcium carbonate).

Stabilizers

Plastics have a reputation for being indestructible, and people worry about them not breaking down when left as litter, so it may be a surprise to know that stabilizers are added to prevent them from breaking down in air, when used as containers of liquids, or when put in sunlight. Just a few parts in a million of an additive will often be enough.

(*Above*) The use of colorants makes this vacuum cleaner both functional and fun to look at.

See **Vol. 6: Dyes, paints, and adhesives** *for more on pigments and coloring.*

See **Vol. 4: Ceramics** *for more on chalk.*

(*Above*) This plastic has been sliced open to show that the color goes all the way through the material.

How plastic items are made

Usually plastic arrives at the factory in the form of pellets, small rodlike pieces of material. They are mixed with any additives that are needed to change the color of the properties of the plastic.

The ingredients are mixed, heated, and stirred. The mixture is most commonly raised above its melting point so that it becomes a liquid. In this form it can be more easily used in automated machines.

Many plastics are shaped by forcing them through a die. This is called EXTRUSION.

(*Above and below*) The world's chemical industry produces well over 40 million tons of ethylene from natural gas and oil every year. Ethylene is the basic building block for many plastics.

(*Below*) Many plastics leave refineries as chips that can be easily and safely transported to a site for melting and forming.

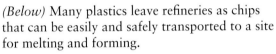

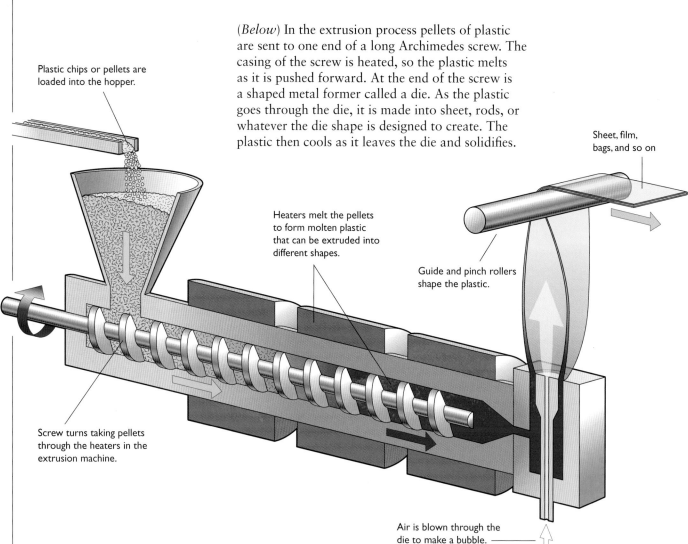

(*Below*) In the extrusion process pellets of plastic are sent to one end of a long Archimedes screw. The casing of the screw is heated, so the plastic melts as it is pushed forward. At the end of the screw is a shaped metal former called a die. As the plastic goes through the die, it is made into sheet, rods, or whatever the die shape is designed to create. The plastic then cools as it leaves the die and solidifies.

Plastic chips or pellets are loaded into the hopper.

Heaters melt the pellets to form molten plastic that can be extruded into different shapes.

Screw turns taking pellets through the heaters in the extrusion machine.

Sheet, film, bags, and so on

Guide and pinch rollers shape the plastic.

Air is blown through the die to make a bubble.

It will produce fibers, sheets, or special shapes (for example, window frames and pipes). Plastic bags are not made as sheets but as tubes that are later welded and cut into bag lengths.

An alternative to extrusion is to force the plastic into a MOLD. That is often done to make complicated shapes. The plastic may be pushed into the mold in the form of a dry powder and heated until it melts. That is called COMPRESSION MOLDING. As the mold is opened, the molded piece is pushed out automatically by pins in the forming part of the molding. That allows high-speed production of molded pieces.

Most molding is done by a process called INJECTION MOLDING, in which the plastic is

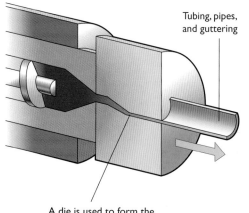

Tubing, pipes, and guttering

A die is used to form the molten plastic into the required shape.

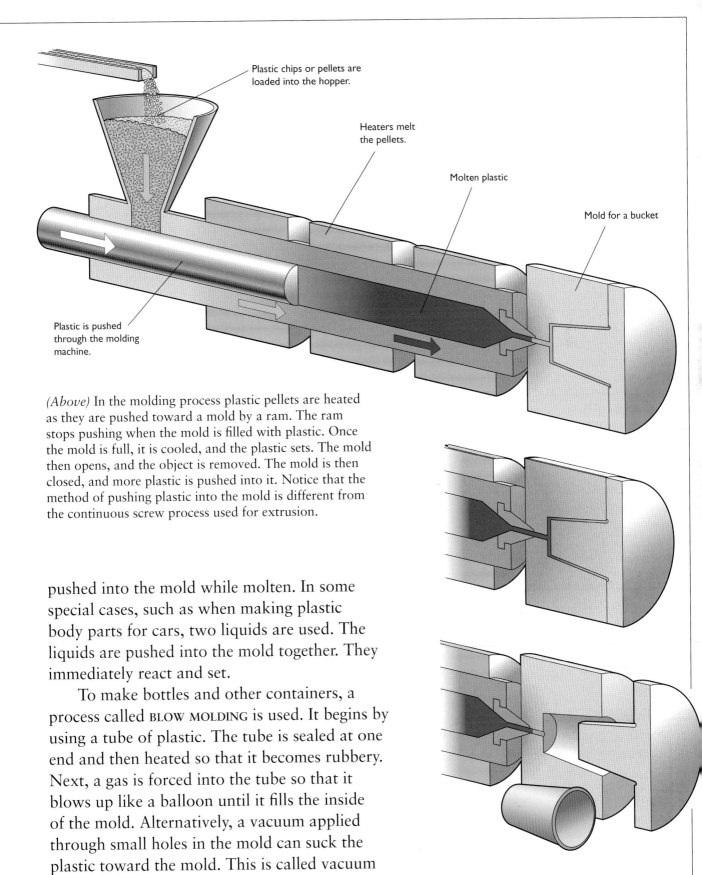

Plastic chips or pellets are loaded into the hopper.

Heaters melt the pellets.

Molten plastic

Mold for a bucket

Plastic is pushed through the molding machine.

(Above) In the molding process plastic pellets are heated as they are pushed toward a mold by a ram. The ram stops pushing when the mold is filled with plastic. Once the mold is full, it is cooled, and the plastic sets. The mold then opens, and the object is removed. The mold is then closed, and more plastic is pushed into it. Notice that the method of pushing plastic into the mold is different from the continuous screw process used for extrusion.

pushed into the mold while molten. In some special cases, such as when making plastic body parts for cars, two liquids are used. The liquids are pushed into the mold together. They immediately react and set.

To make bottles and other containers, a process called BLOW MOLDING is used. It begins by using a tube of plastic. The tube is sealed at one end and then heated so that it becomes rubbery. Next, a gas is forced into the tube so that it blows up like a balloon until it fills the inside of the mold. Alternatively, a vacuum applied through small holes in the mold can suck the plastic toward the mold. This is called vacuum forming. The mold is kept cold so that as the

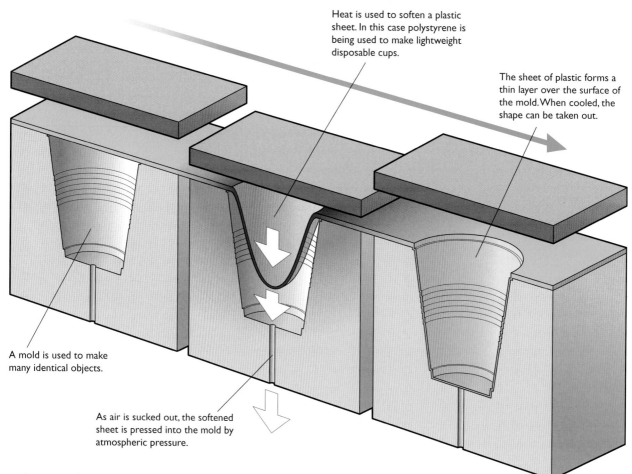

Heat is used to soften a plastic sheet. In this case polystyrene is being used to make lightweight disposable cups.

The sheet of plastic forms a thin layer over the surface of the mold. When cooled, the shape can be taken out.

A mold is used to make many identical objects.

As air is sucked out, the softened sheet is pressed into the mold by atmospheric pressure.

(Above) In the vacuum forming process a plastic sheet travels over the top of a set of molds. Heat is applied, and the sheet softens and sags down into the mold. A vacuum is then used to suck the air from between the plastic and the mold, and ordinary air pressure then forces the sagged plastic sheet to fit the shape of the mold. The heat is removed, and the vacuum-formed plastic sets can be removed.

plastic touches the mold, it cools and becomes solid again. A common plastic used for clear bottles such as those used for soft drinks is PET (see page 50). As it happens, in this case the stretching process also has the effect of strengthening the material.

Because PET is a thermoplastic and can be reheated, PET bottles can be recycled.

Other materials used for plastic bottles include polyethylene (see page 28), polypropylene (see page 31), and PVC (see page 35). The exact material used may depend on the liquid that the bottle is to contain.

If plastic is used for eyeglasses, a thermoset is used because it would be undesirable for the lenses to change shape as they warmed. The plastic lenses are made by pouring the thermoset liquid into a hot mold. The hot mold causes chemical reactions to take place in the thermoset, which then hardens.

Completely hollow articles such as balls are made by putting a liquid into a mold and then spinning it so that the liquid is thrown to the outside of the mold. When it is cooled or heated (depending on the plastic), the plastic sets.

Dipping

Some plastics can be formed into products by dipping a mold into a bath of the liquid. The liquid is cold and contains special plasticizers. After the mold is dipped into the liquid, it is taken out and heated. The heating causes a chemical reaction that makes the liquid into a rubbery solid. "Rubber" gloves are typical of products made this way using low-porosity PVC.

(*Above*) Polystyrene can be made transparent and used for cups.

Foams

Foams are an important category of plastic because the air trapped inside them makes a good insulator. Foams also tend to be stronger and more rigid. But at the same time, the bubbles in the foam will collapse if the foam is pressed hard. That can be an advantage. It absorbs the shock of a blow, for example, when foam is used as protective packaging. Polystyrene, polyurethane, and phenol formaldehyde are the main plastics used in this way.

(*Below*) Protective packaging used to ensure safe transportation of fragile items.

Gases other than air can be used. The materials used for producing gases can be mixed up with the plastic and then heated to a temperature at which they turn to gas. As a result, the bubbles form throughout the plastic. The gas must not be explosive or react in any way. The gas most commonly produced is nitrogen.

The amount of foaming can be spectacular. One gram of a substance called azodicarbonamide, when added to 100 grams of polyethylene, expands to a foam of over 800 cubic centimeters. Cans of foaming agent are used to seal gaps in building work.

Furniture cushions are made of a plastic (polyether, see page 54) that is a thermoset because it must keep its shape when in a warm room. In this case the plastic is mixed with a liquid that turns into a gas when it is warmed. At the same time, the thermoset reacts and hardens, so that the bubbles remain even though the gas eventually evaporates. The resulting foam has a permanent springiness.

Polyesters (see page 50) treated in the same way produce rigid foams. They are used for packaging.

How plastics are joined

Plastics can be joined by ADHESIVES, or they can be welded. Welding is used, for example, in the manufacture of polyethylene bags. A long tube of material goes along a machine, and hot metal bars press down on it at intervals. The hot bars cause the upper and lower surface of the plastic tube to weld together.

Decorative laminates

A plastic may not have all the properties that are needed for a job, or its use may be too expensive. For these and many other reasons it is common to make a sandwich of several different types of material. It is called a LAMINATE.

Plywood is a common example of a laminate. It consists of sheets of wood interleaved with sheets of resin (plastic).

Many kitchen work surfaces are also laminates. They are molded onto a chipboard or other base of cheap, hard material. The surface laminate is made of sheets of paper, the top one of which carries the color or pattern that will be seen. All of the sheets are soaked in a thermosetting resin (melamine-formaldehyde). That is why many work surfaces are described as "melamine" (see page 45).

(*Above and above right*) Polyethylene is an adhesive. It can also be foamed by adding a propellant under pressure. Once expanded and set, it can be cut and sawn or painted like wood.

(*Below*) Rigid foams can be used for a variety of purposes, including flower arranging.

Laminated windshields are also laminates of plastic and glass.

Reinforcing a plastic

Plastics have a huge number of desirable features; but despite this, they may not always be strong enough. To help improve strength, especially when plastics are used as thin sheets or rods, they are reinforced with fibers.

In a material such as fiberglass you may think that the glass is the main component, and it is simply stuck together by some form of glue. In fact, fiberglass is a reinforced thermosetting resin. So fiberglass should really be called glass fiber-reinforced resin. What the glass fibers do is spread any stresses across the whole resin and so prevent it from cracking. That allows the resin to be used in smaller quantities, as, for example, in the hulls of canoes (see page 53).

(*Below*) Foamed polystyrene makes a good insulator and is widely used in disposable cups. However, if the cups are simply thrown away, the environment may suffer.

Recycling a plastic

Plastics make up 9.5% of our trash by weight, while paper constitutes 38.9%, and glass and metals make up 13.9%.

Many people think that plastics are indestructible. We see so much of it surviving in trash when other materials, such as paper, have rotted away. So, with such huge quantities of plastics being produced, it becomes vital to find ways of RECYCLING (reusing) the plastics after we have used them.

The difficulty in recycling plastics is that you need to know the plastic you are dealing with if you are to reuse it successfully. Mixed plastics generally cannot be recycled. Most recycling of plastics has therefore centered on thermoplastics, such as containers like plastic bottles. Thermoplastics can be recycled easily if they are mainly made of one material and so can be easily sorted.

Thermosetting plastics are extremely difficult to recycle because when they are heated, they simply decompose. Thermoplastic plastics, on the other hand, will melt.

It is striking how so many different plastics are used to make the same or similar items. Several plastics can be manufactured in transparent or opaque, hard or flexible forms. That is particularly the case with the common plastics and makes them very difficult to identify—which is why we need marks to tell them apart. For example, you will find a triangle containing the number 4 and the letters PET on the side or base of most plastic beverage bottles. However, the mark does not completely solve the problem, because it is possible to make a wide variety of plastics with the same chemical formula. You can see this in the example of a plastic food tray. It is made of polystyrene; but to get it to hold its shape well, the polystyrene is made with a high density. The same material is also used to make disposable knives and forks, but they are made with a lower density because it is easier to mold such polystyrene using injection machines. If these materials are brought together and mixed, they cannot be used again for their original purpose because the mix has been contaminated. Furthermore, each might have been colored with a different pigment. Again, that adds to the difficulty of finding a reuse for the mixed material.

(*Right*) In some developing countries people can even scrape out a living by sorting plastics for recycling.

(*Below*) Many traffic cones are made from mixed recycled plastic.

In general, recycled plastics are used in places where quality is not as important as in the original use. Plastic PET bottles, for example, can be melted down and spun into fiber that can be used for cheap pillows. Recycled PVC can be used to make traffic cones. Mixed plastics can be used to make a solid base for floors.

If all other recycling fails, the material can be burned, in which case it releases heat that can be used in power plants. That is what has to be done with plastics that are soiled by food (such as food wrap) or by people (such as diapers).

When plastics are burned, they can be used to help other trash, such as wet trash, burn too. Care has to be taken, however, to make sure that toxic fumes are not produced during the process.

(*Above*) The bottom of this plastic container shows a recycling symbol. It follows the Resin Identification Code shown on page 26. In this case it is made of polyethylene terephthalate (PET or PETE)

Resin Identification Code

To make it easier to recycle plastics, the Society of the Plastics Industry, Inc., introduced a voluntary resin identification coding system. The codes are shown below. You can find the symbols on many plastics products. Many other countries use a somewhat similar system, but you may not find a number; instead, just the code letters, such as PP, are given.

Polyethylene terephthalate (PET or PETE)

Low-density polyethylene (LDPE)

Low-density polyethylene storage container lid (LDPE)

High-density polyethylene (HDPE)

Polypropylene (PP)

Polypropylene chemical bottle (HDPE)

Transparent polypropylene storage container (PP)

Polyvinyl chloride (PVC)

Polystyrene (PS)

Transparent colored polystyrene (PS)

"Popcorn" polystyrene (PS)

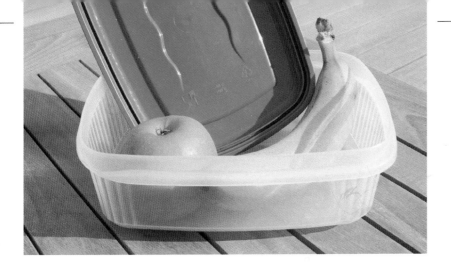

(*Left and below*) This food storage container is polypropylene (PP) with a low-density polyethylene (LDPE) lid. It shows clearly how a combination of materials is often used in constructing a product. The lid needs to be more flexible than the base so that it can be drawn over it to form a tight snap-on seal.

2: Common plastics

Although there are many thousands of plastics, each fits within a small number of basic types. Furthermore, many of the huge range of plastics we have invented are not in common use because they have only specialized (although often important) applications. As a result, most common objects are made from a surprisingly small range of plastics. In this section we will look in more detail at some of them, their main properties, and how they are used in some of the things we buy.

The main types of polymers used

There is a fundamental difference between plastics (polymers) that have a long central chain (or backbone) consisting only of carbon links, and those in which oxygen, nitrogen, sulfur, and silicon are also part of the backbone.

Carbon backbone polymers are made by adding extra units to their length, a process called ADDITION POLYMERIZATION. It is of most importance to plastics that are molded.

Simple plastics

Plastics with simple carbon links are often collectively known as VINYLS or vinyl compounds.

The common source for all of these plastics is in natural gas and crude oil. They are refined to make ethylene, propylene, and butene. These are materials with simple structures that can be used to create the polymers. Although you may not have heard of these starting products, you will certainly have heard of the finished products, as detailed below.

Polyethylene and similar

There is one group of plastics that stands head and shoulders above all of the rest in terms of its widespread use for the things we have around us. This group is built on a single chain of carbon and hydrogen bonded together. It is polyethylene.

(*Below*) Transparent polyethylene bag made of LDPE.

(*Below*) Garbage cans can be made from polyethylene and contain carbon to protect the plastic from light damage.

(*Above and below*) Carrier bags and garbage bags are mainly made from LDPE.

Polyethylene (LDPE and HDPE)

Hans von Pechmann, a German chemist, made the first small amount of polyethylene in 1899. For the next six decades it would have little obvious widespread use.

In 1935 the British chemists Eric Fawcett and Reginald Gibson took polyethylene a step further by making it into a white, waxy solid. In this form it had a small and specialized range of uses, being made primarily into insulators in radar wires. It was only in 1963 that Karl Ziegler in Germany found ways to make it a more widely usable product.

Today, polyethylene is used everywhere. The advantages of all polyethylenes are: light weight, formable into any shape, toughness, ease of processing, chemical resistance, abrasion resistance, electrical resistance (it is a good insulator), impact resistance, low coefficient of friction (it is quite slippery), near-zero moisture absorption, easy to work with using ordinary machines, and can be heat welded.

There are two main forms of polyethylene (PE), low-density and high-density. Low-density polyethylene (LDPE) is an excellent material where flexibility and corrosion resistance are important, but where stiffness, high temperature, and structural strength are not important. It is used to make almost every packaging film, trash bag, and grocery bag. It is also used for chemical-resistant tanks and containers, food storage containers, and moisture barriers (it is placed between the soil and the concrete slab used to make a house floor). Most things that are flexible, such as a squeezable bottle or toy, are made from LDPE.

By adding sulfur and chlorine, polyethylene can be made to resemble rubber, giving it resistance to light, ozone, flames, and oils. Most "rubber" bands, belts, and "rubber" hoses are not rubber at all, but a form of LDPE.

High-density polyethylene (HDPE) is made at very low temperatures and pressures, allowing the chains to pack more closely together than in LDPE. In this form it is used for bottle tops, bowls, buckets, plastic milk bottles, food cutting boards, corrosion-resistant wall coverings, lavatory partitions, radiation shielding, self-supporting containers, and any other place where a more rigid, opaque (not transparent) plastic is needed. It is even used for some industrial "hard hats."

HPDE is more rigid than LDPE. It is four times as strong as LDPE when pulled and three times as strong when squashed. Moisture and water (including salt water) have no effect on HDPE.

(*Below*) Because HDPE has good chemical resistance, it is used for packaging many household as well as industrial chemicals such as bleach and detergents.

Pigmented HDPE bottles generally have better stress, crack, and chemical resistance than bottles made from unpigmented HDPE.

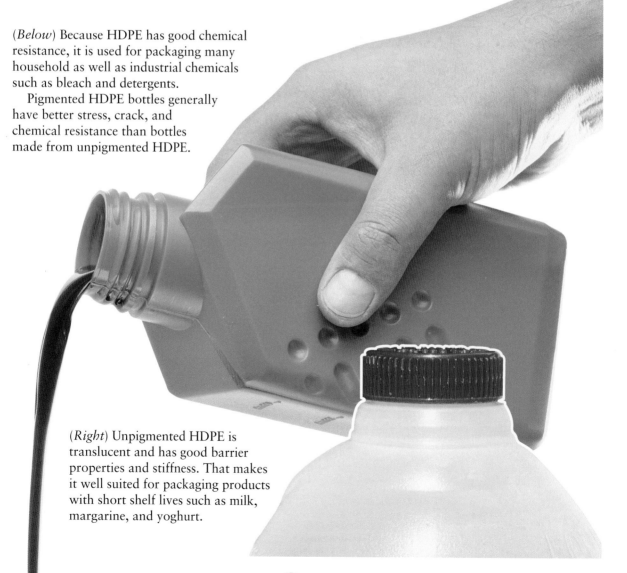

(*Right*) Unpigmented HDPE is translucent and has good barrier properties and stiffness. That makes it well suited for packaging products with short shelf lives such as milk, margarine, and yoghurt.

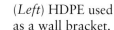

(*Left*) HDPE used as a wall bracket.

(*Below*) Plastic buckets are HDPE.

Polypropylene (PP)

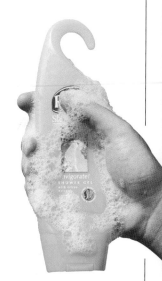

PP is not unlike PE, but it melts at a higher temperature, it is harder, and is not as flexible. Much of it is made into fibers, and in this form it finds widespread uses from diapers to the fabrics used in road construction. It melts at too low a temperature to be ironed and so is not used in ordinary clothing.

Polypropylene is a cheap material that offers a combination of outstanding physical, chemical, mechanical, thermal, and electrical properties not found in any other thermoplastic. It is light in weight, resistant to staining, and has a low moisture

5 PP

(*Above*) Shampoo bottle and many other squeezy containers are often made of PP.

absorption rate. Compared to low- or high-density polyethylene, it has a lower impact strength, but softens at higher temperatures and is stronger. As a result, it is ideal for carrying hot (not boiling) liquids or gases.

PP can be blow molded into a wide variety of shapes and is found in plastic bottles for food, shampoos, household cleaners, and also in some rigid containers. Its softening point is higher than for PE, and it is the material made into dishwasher-proof plastic containers.

It is also injection molded into many products, such as toys, automobile battery casings, and outdoor furniture. It will also withstand flexing without breaking, and so it has been used in containers that need plastic hinges, such as lunch boxes.

Ethylene-propylene is a compound used to make the insulation of electrical wires.

(*Above and below*) Polypropylene has excellent chemical resistance, is strong, and has the lowest density of the plastics used in packaging, making it ideal for battery casings and chemical bottles.

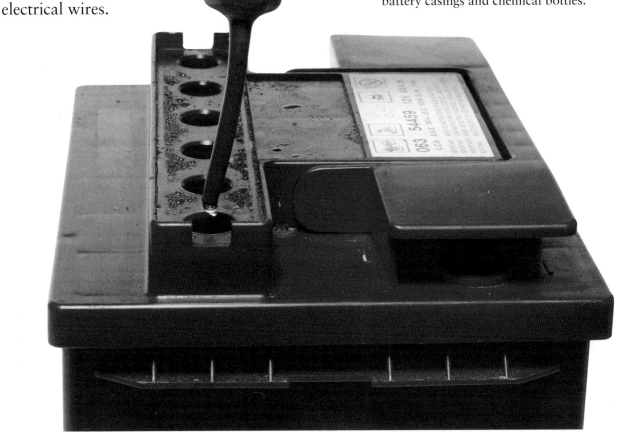

32

(*Left and below*) Polypropylene will withstand flexing, and so it is used for plastic hinges.

Polystyrene (PS)

Polystyrene is much more brittle than the plastics listed above. It is made from ethylene and benzene gases.

It was discovered in 1839 by Eduard Simon in Germany, but a use for it was only found in 1938.

The structure of PS contains big rings of molecules, which makes it impossible for the molecules to pack closely together. As a result, the material always has a low density and feels lightweight.

PS can be foamed, and in this form it has very wide applications in packaging. It is often called styrofoam. Many disposable cups, plates, and trays are made of PS. PS can be opaque or transparent. In its transparent form it is used, for example, for CD "jewel boxes."

6 PS

(*Below*) General purpose polystyrene is clear and hard, making it suitable for transparent rulers. It can be colored to produce attractive casings such as this CD case.

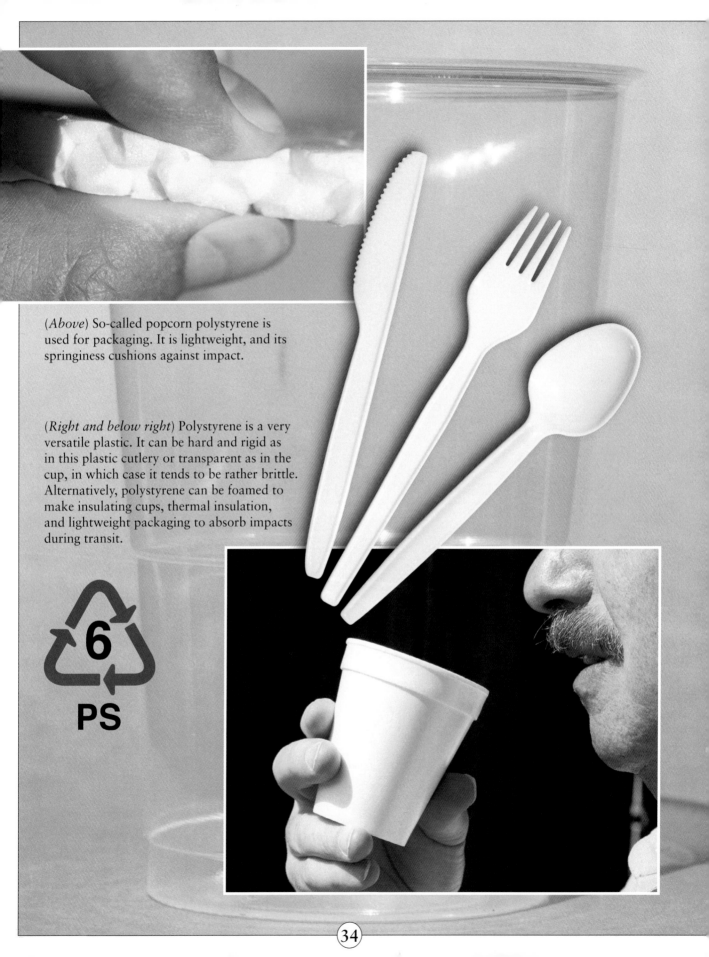

(*Above*) So-called popcorn polystyrene is used for packaging. It is lightweight, and its springiness cushions against impact.

(*Right and below right*) Polystyrene is a very versatile plastic. It can be hard and rigid as in this plastic cutlery or transparent as in the cup, in which case it tends to be rather brittle. Alternatively, polystyrene can be foamed to make insulating cups, thermal insulation, and lightweight packaging to absorb impacts during transit.

6

PS

(*Right*) Old 78 records are PVC, as are the plant holders that can be made from them if the vinyl is soaked in hot water.

Vinyl (polyvinyl chloride, or PVC)

PVC is the second great giant of the plastics world. It is made from ethylene, oxygen, and hydrogen chloride.

PVC was discovered by Eugen Baumann in Germany in 1872, but for half a century it was not used because it was too rigid. In 1926 a "plasticized" version was made, which was much more flexible. As a result, it became the standard material for "vinyl" records.

PVC is a thermoplastic and so can be heated and reformed, as many people have discovered when they make old 78 records into vases and plant pots!

The advantages of PVC are its high strength, that it is cheap to produce, it doesn't shrink or swell, it has good weather resistance, it has high impact strength, it is easy to color, it is chemically inert, it is easy to work with, and it is tasteless, odorless, nontoxic, and a good insulator.

(*Left*) Some windows and siding are made of a form of PVC.

(*Left and below*) PVC inflatable bed and play castles.

(*Above*) PVC is used for drain pipes.

(*Below*) Nearly all plastic drainage pipes are PVC. This is the view under a kitchen sink, showing the piping that carries the waste from the sink.

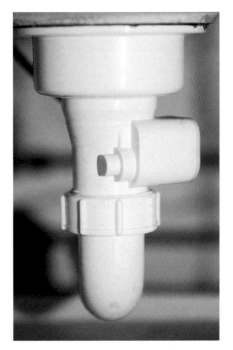

(*Above*) A form of PVC is used for windows and doors because it is weatherproof and needs no maintenance.

(*Above*) PVDC is used to make cling wrap.

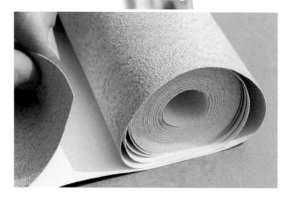

(*Left*) Flexible hoses are made of a reinforced PVC.

Modern PVC is used widely in building. Most rigid plastic water pipes and waste pipes are made of PVC. A light-resistant version (sometimes called uPVC) has been developed for window frames and siding. Many wires are insulated with PVC.

It can also be made more flexible, and in this form it is used in garden hoses, imitation leather upholstery on cheap furniture, and floor covering (imitation linoleum). It is also used for the heavier kind of shower curtain.

A variant called PVDC will not allow gases or water vapor through, and that has made it a favorite material for cling wrap and other kinds of transparent food packaging. It is also used for pool liners, sprinkler systems, and wall coverings (washable wallpaper).

Rigid PVC is easily machined, it can be heat formed and welded, and it can even be glued, something that is unusual among plastics. PVC can be both painted or printed on. This again is unusual. Stiff PVC is made in rods, sheets, slabs, pipes, and tubular bars.

(*Above*) Washable (vinyl) wallpaper.

Polyvinyl acetate (PVAc)

PVAc is made from ethylene, oxygen, and acetic acid. It is used in liquid rather than solid form, for instance, as the polymer used to carry the pigment (coloring) in water-based paints. It also makes a very sticky adhesive, found as white glue or PVA glue, where it is mostly used for joining wooden parts.

When slightly altered in composition and made into a solid film, it is used as the plastic in laminated safety windshields, door glazing, and shop windows.

(*Above*) This is PVA glue, often used to glue pieces of wood together. Here it is being applied to a dowel that will be fitted into holes in two pieces of wood, giving the strength of both the wooden peg and the adhesive.

See **Vol. 6: Dyes, paints, and adhesives**

(*Below*) Many cycling helmets are made of ABS. (The visor is acrylic.)

(*Left*) ABS is commonly used for computer casings.

ABS (Acrylonitrile-butadiene-styrene)

ABS is a special form of vinyl called a copolymer, meaning it is made of styrene and other kinds of polymer. ABS plastic is rigid, tough, and impact and heat resistant. As a result, it is used where these properties are of great importance. For example, computer casings need to be heat and fire resistant and also stand up to blows. ABS is also made into rigid luggage and sports helmets, and used when impact resistance is needed. Because it is not flexible, it is not used, however, when the material needs to absorb slight shocks, such as car bumpers.

Acrylic plastics

Acrylics are rigid transparent plastics. Acrylics were among the first plastics ever put to use. The first acrylic was made by Georg Kahlbaum in Switzerland in 1880, and it was put into commercial production as early as 1927. A more rigid form was developed in England by Rowland Hill and John Crawford, and given the name Perspex®. In 1931 sheets were used for laminated safety glass and given the name Plexiglas®.

(*Left*) Perspex® can be used as a glass substitute, as here in this poolside table. Over time, however, it will become scuffed and also lose a little of its transparency.

(*Left*) Perspex® can be used as a decorative plastic, as in the case of this salt grinder.

(*Above and below*) Acrylic fibers are widely used as a wool substitute. They can also be made flame resistant.

See **Vol. 7: Fibers** *for more on acrylic fibers.*

A variation of acrylic plastic was produced in America in 1950 and made into an acrylic fiber called Orlon®. From this began the widespread use of acrylic fibers in clothing.

Acrylic will not take up dyes and so cannot be used alone if a colored material is needed. However, when combined with very small amounts of vinyl acetate, it produces soft fibers that will take a dye, and that closely resemble wool. Acrylic fibers are used to replace wool in socks, sweaters, and carpets because they cost far less than wool. They also are immune to attack by moths.

By adding chlorine, the fiber can be made flame resistant and so can be used for children's wear.

The advantages of acrylics are that they are half the weight of glass, they are impact resistant, and they are only affected by sun and salt spray after prolonged exposure, at which point they tend to turn yellow and become far more brittle. However, because acrylics are relatively soft and can be dissolved by plastic solvents, they cannot be cleaned by many window cleaning sprays, scouring compounds, acetone, gasoline, benzene, carbon tetrachloride, or lacquer thinner, all of which either scratch the surface or dissolve it.

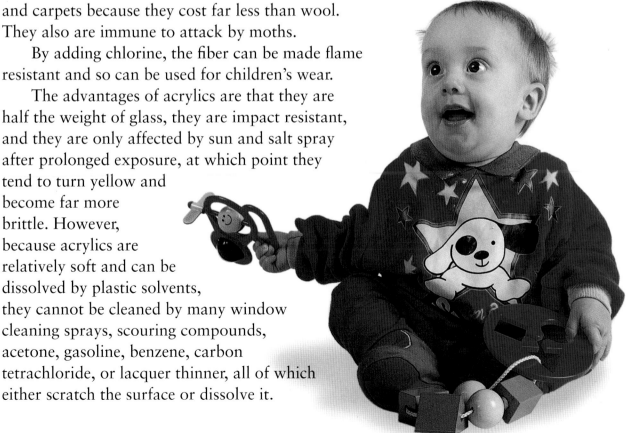

(*Above, right, and below*) Polymethyl methacrylate is used for instrument panels and aircraft windows.

Polymethyl methacrylate (PMMA)

PMMA is a transparent, rigid plastic that does not change with exposure to sunlight. It is, however, more expensive than common acrylic.

PMMA is used as a specialized glass substitute, for lighted advertising displays, for instrument panels, and for skylights, aircraft windows, and automobile side and rear light clusters.

A variation of this material, made suitably soft, is used to make contact lenses.

Cyanoacrylate changes into a strong adhesive when exposed to the moisture in air. It is the material that makes many contact adhesives such as super glue. This substance readily sticks skin

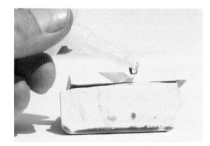

(*Above*) Super glue is a cyanoacrylate.

(*Right*) PTFE tape is used in plumbing because it can be formed into a thin, rubbery tape.

See **Vol. 6: Dyes, paints, and adhesives** *for more on super glue and other adhesives.*

(*Below*) PTFE as Teflon® is a common nonstick surface in cookware.

together—very useful for some medical procedures, but of great danger to super glue users.

Polymethyl acrylate and polyethyl acrylate are also used as adhesives or added to materials intended for making coatings that have to stick to surfaces. Acrylic paints are one example of this.

Polytetrafluoroethylene (PTFE)

By adding the element fluorine to ethylene, a range of nonstick plastics can be produced. PTFE is nonstick because the fluorine atoms that surround the carbon chain bond very tightly to the carbon atoms and so make it chemically unreactive.

These polymers were discovered by Roy Plunkett in America in 1938. In 1960 PTFE was sold as a nonstick coating called Teflon®. It is now found on a large number of cookware products.

It is also used very widely to help machinery parts move, where it coats bearings that need no oil as a lubrication. Made into a tape, it is also used to replace plumbers' putty and makes a watertight seal in screwed plumbing joints.

Diene plastics

Dienes are a range of plastics in which pairs of bonded carbon atoms occur. They are mostly used as a substitute for rubber in automotive tires. Because the materials have a natural springiness, they are also used in footwear.

Neoprene, a synthetic rubber, is in this group. It is widely used to make sealing O-rings in machinery.

Styrene-butadiene rubber with carbon black added is strong and resists wear. For this reason it is widely used in automobile tires and footwear, and also as a rubbery adhesive in upholstery and footwear. In adhesive form it can be used as a hot glue.

(*Below*) Tires often contain carbon black and styrene-butadiene. Sidewalls need to be flexible and contain one part natural rubber by weight, one part butadiene rubber, and one part carbon black. Tire tread composition is different. It contains no natural rubber at all but two parts styrene-butadiene rubber, one part butadiene rubber, and two parts carbon black.

(*Above*) Neoprene is used for hammers when the hammer blows must not mark the surface, such as in self-assembly of shelves.

(*Left*) Springy footwear insoles being stamped from sheets of styrene-butadiene rubber.

Complex plastics

As we have seen, plastics with only carbon in their backbones are called addition polymers, that is, one carbon unit adds to another to form a long chain. They are mainly thermoplastics. However, there is another and very important group in which several different components come together by a process known as CONDENSATION POLYMERIZATION. This produces plastics in which there is oxygen, nitrogen, sulfur, or silicon as well as carbon in the backbone chain. They are much more complicated than the carbon backbone chains but have many important uses. They are mainly thermosets.

Phenols

Phenols are an important thermosetting group of plastics. They are excellent insulators, rigid and easy to machine into new shapes, and lightweight. They resist heat and abrasion, are corrosion resistant, have good strength, resist moisture, and do not change size much when heated or cooled.

As it happens, one of the first plastics ever made was a phenolic resin. Indeed, people often think that Bakelite, marketed in 1907, marks the beginning of the plastics industry. That is because, although simple carbon chain plastics had been discovered before this time, Leo Baekeland was the first person to find a way of using and, just as importantly, marketing plastic. He called his plastic Bakelite.

Diene plastics can be used for rubber bands, rubber gaskets, and O-ring seals.

(*Above*) This old hairdryer is made from Bakelite.

(*Right*) Phenols are heat-resistant thermosets widely used for pan handles.

43

(*Above*) Phenolic resin is used in sticking the laminates of plywood together.

See **Vol. 3: Wood and paper** *for more on wood and particleboard.*

(*Below*) The clear protective surface coat on a car contains melamine.

(*Below*) Melamine picnic mug.

Materials like Bakelite were first used for cabinets and other objects that needed to be molded. Because of its excellent insulating properties, the resin was made into sockets, knobs and dials for radios, and even spark-plug caps in cars.

Today, these kinds of substances are rarely used for such purposes, but instead are applied primarily as adhesives. Phenols can be used to join wood by forming chemical bonds with the hard part of the wood called lignin. That is why, when a wood joint glued with a phenolic resin breaks, it does not break through the glue but to one side or the other, since the glue is stronger than the wood.

Phenolic resins are also used to stick together sheets of plywood and to attach the particles of wood in particle board. However, because the glue is dark and can stain the wood, it is not used where appearance is critical (see instead PVA on page 37). Many plastic cookware handles are made of phenolic resin reinforced with fibers.

Phenolic sheet (such as used on tabletops) is a hard, dense material made by applying heat and pressure to layers of paper or glass cloth impregnated with synthetic resin. These layers of laminations are usually of cellulose paper, cotton fabrics, synthetic yarn fabrics, glass fabrics, or unwoven fabrics. When heat and pressure are applied to the layers, polymerization transforms the layers into a high-pressure thermosetting industrial laminated plastic that is often called Formica®.

Urea

Resins based on a substance called urea have much the same properties as those based on phenols. However, they are a lighter color and so can be used for joining wood when the results might be seen. It is not as weather resistant as phenol glue and so is best used indoors.

(*Left*) Melamine used as kitchen surface.

When used with fabrics, they help produce noniron, crease-resistant properties. They are also blended with some paints to make them harder and so resist wear better.

Melamine

Resins based on melamine are harder than resins based on urea, and for this reason they are used for hard picnic cups and plates.

Because of its hardness, melamine is also used in surface coatings that need to be very abrasion resistant. The surface "lacquer" coating used to protect the paint on a car contains melamine.

(*Above*) Formica tabletops are melamine. They can be manufactured with a range of colors and patterns. It is even possible to add texture to mimic wood.

(*Above*) Celluloid goggles used in World War II.

Cellulose

Cellulose is a natural plastic. It is found in every plant, where it makes up the main fibers in stems and leaves. It is the material that produces cotton and flax, for example. Paper is made from cellulose. Cellulose is a thermosetting plastic.

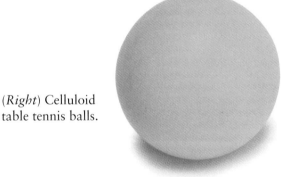

(*Right*) Celluloid table tennis balls.

See **Vol. 7: Fibers** *for more on cellulose.*

The development of cellulose began in 1861 when Alexander Parkes in England produced Parkesine, perhaps the first plastic. In 1869 John W. Hyatt in America made this kind of plastic on a commercial scale—the first person in the world to do so. It was called CELLULOID and molded into shapes that were then marketed as artificial ivory. It was used for piano keys and for the then fashionable stiff collars and cuffs. Later it was used for movie film. It could also be made into a substitute for tortoiseshell and used for combs and cases. It was later used for side windows in cars. However, it readily caught fire. So, when safer products like Bakelite came along, celluloid use declined. It still remains in production for table tennis balls and nail polish.

(*Above*) This old radio case is made of celluloid designed to look like tortoiseshell.

See **Vol. 7: Fibers** *for more on rayon.*

The first fiber to be produced was reconstituted cellulose. It was made by Louis-Marie-Hilaire Bernigaud in France in 1889. Production began in 1891, and in 1924 it was named RAYON.

Yet another type of fibrous cellulose was developed by Charles Cross, Edward Bevan, and Clayton Beadle in England. It was produced in 1905 and is now known as VISCOSE. Today, it is the most widely used form of cellulose.

Cellulose diacetate was used in 1921 in England as a soft and silky fiber. Eventually it became known by the trademarks Tricel and Arnel. They were the first drip-dry fabrics, and they were also almost noniron.

They have now largely been replaced by polyester fibers, which are cheaper to make and have the same properties. The main use of Tricel and Arnel now is for the shiny lining material in coats.

Cellophane is made from cellulose and extruded in sheet form. Acetate film is another cellulose-based plastic.

(*Below*) Cellophane wrapping around a disposable polystyrene cup.

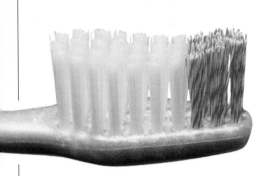

(*Above*) Nylon is hardwearing, flexible, and does not rot when wet and so can be used for toothbrush bristles.

(*Below*) Safety gloves made of Kevlar®.

Nylon

Nylon is a fiber made from a plastic known as a polyamide. It was the first synthetic fiber ever produced (rayon being a natural fiber). It was made by DuPont in America in 1938 and did not use natural cellulose as a starting point.

Nylon shrinks and swells as temperature changes, about three times as much as aluminum, for example. On the other hand, it is hard but not as strong as metal. Kevlar® is a derivative of nylon. Unlike ordinary nylon, Kevlar® is five times stronger than steel by weight and is hard enough to resist knives and bullets. As a result, it is used in protective wear. It is also used in flame-resistant protective clothing for firefighters and racecar drivers.

Nylon is widely used because of its strength and wear resistance. It has good heat resistance, it is not affected by most chemicals, but it changes size considerably when it gets wet and is quite expensive to make. It is preferred, for example, for soft-sided luggage, for socks, and to make carpets more hardwearing. It is also used for gears in electric motors and for bearings, fishing line, toothbrushes, sports equipment, and zippers.

(*Right and below*) Nylon thread has many uses. It is tough and durable. It is also slow to rot and so is used for poolside carpeting and fishing lines.

However, in the case of fishing lines the fact that it will not decompose in water means that snagged lines stay a threat to wildlife such as geese and swans for a long time.

Polyesters

Polyesters are a very important group of plastics whose uses range from fibers to sheet and bottles.

See **Vol. 7: Fibers** *for much more on nylon, rayon, and other plastics used as fibers.*

Polyethylene terephthalate (PET or PETE)

PET is a very common product that has an enormous range of applications. Your clothes probably contain polyester, and you mainly drink soft drinks from a polyester bottle.

PET was discovered by J. Rex Whinfield and James T. Dickson in England in 1940. It was trademarked as Terylene®. It was also developed independently in America and produced in 1953 by DuPont under the trademark of Dacron®.

PET is quite stiff and strong, and resists changes in its shape. That is why PET bottles bounce back into shape after they have been squeezed. It also has high waterproof and gas penetration properties. That is why it is widely used for carbonated beverages (fizzy drinks).

PET can be injection molded to make bottles, but it can also be drawn out into fibers. Fibers produced from PET, manufactured under the general name of polyester, are among the most commonly used in the garment industry. It is the most important of the synthetic fibers. They also go under such names as Dacron® and Terylene®.

(*Above*) Polyester fibers are very versatile and are used in both everyday clothes and for specialized outdoor wear.

(*Below*) A piece of mixed nylon and viscose cloth used for making clothes.

(*Below*) PET is the base for videotape cases.

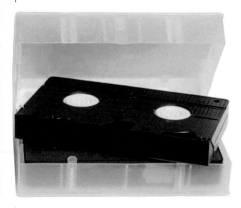

(*Left*) PET is often used in squeezable containers.

(*Below*) A clear PET bottle used to contain a carbonated drink.

The stiffness of polyester produces the wrinkle-resisting (known as stay-pressed) properties of many clothes. They are not necessarily used alone, but often combined with softer fibers such as rayon, wool, and cotton. That increases both the stay-pressed property and comfort of a garment. Polyester can also be made into fiber fillings for pillows and quilts, and it is widely used in carpets.

The strength of polyester means that it is useful as an industrial yarn in making tires, as a reinforcement for garden hoses, and as safety belts in cars. In factories it is also used in many drive belts as well as in the surface layer of diapers and disposable clothing. A more dense form of PET is used as the base for tape in tape and video recorders.

PET is also a recyclable plastic. That is why you are encouraged to put out plastic bottles separately from other trash, and why PET products have a special recycle mark on them (see page 25).

Polycarbonate (PC)

Polycarbonate is a very stiff, cheap form of polyester that will stand up to hard blows better than almost any other kind of plastic. Unnotched polycarbonate is virtually unbreakable. That makes it useful for many external applications, such as bumpers on cars and also antivandal light fixtures. Polycarbonate is also used for safety helmets.

Polycarbonate will not soften in heat, so products keep their shape when heated. That is another reason why polycarbonate can be used for lamp housings.

Polycarbonate products can be painted, printed, or have a metal coating added in a vacuum chamber. They can also be treated so that they will not discolor in sunlight.

Some polycarbonate is very transparent and can be used as a substitute for glass. It is used for pressure windows, face shields, street and public building furniture (for example, lamps), sunroofs, and other places needing protection from the weather but with light able to get in. In the case of skylights double-skinned polycarbonate is used because then

(*Above*) Compact disks are polycarbonate.

(*Below*) Polycarbonate vandal-resistant light fixture.

it also acts as an insulator. Polycarbonate makes the disk material of a compact disk.

Polyester paints and resins

Polyesters are widely used in paints. They are very complicated substances that are oil based, using oils such as linseed oil. When an oil-based polyester paint is applied to a surface, the oil reacts with the oxygen from the air to produce a new, hard surface. We normally call this "drying," although it is not a loss of water but a chemical reaction. Polyester forms the bulk of the paint, being mixed with a coloring material (a pigment) and a solvent such as spirits to make it easier to apply the paint.

Polyesters without oil are used as coating materials. They are often polyesters combined with alcohol and can be used with other plastics such as melamine. In this form they may be called lacquers and are used as clear coating on, for example, car bodies.

Polyesters can be used as the resin that binds the glass in glass fiber. Glass fiber is used widely for canoes, boat hulls, and shower trays.

A range of adhesives will stick together pieces of polycarbonate. Epoxy, urethane, and silicone can all be used.

See **Vol. 6: Dyes, paints, and adhesives** for more on polyester paints.

(*Below*) Polyesters provide the resin that makes the bulk of the material in glass fiber. The combination of resins and thin glass fibers used in a canoe provides a material that is thin enough to be translucent yet strong enough to hold the weight of a person.

Polyethers

Polyethers are plastics made by joining atoms to a backbone unit made of two carbon atoms and an oxygen atom.

They can be blended with, for example, polystyrene to produce a high-strength, moisture-resistant plastic. One use is for the plastic hubcaps of some cars. However, because the plastic does not take color well, the plastic has to be painted. That is why some hubcaps reveal a different color underneath when they are scratched.

Because they resist fire, they have found many uses as cabinets for electrical and electronic equipment, especially in factories and offices. Some are used as housings for electrical sockets.

(*Above*) Some wall sockets are made of polyether.

(*Below*) A two-tube epoxy resin being mixed as an adhesive.

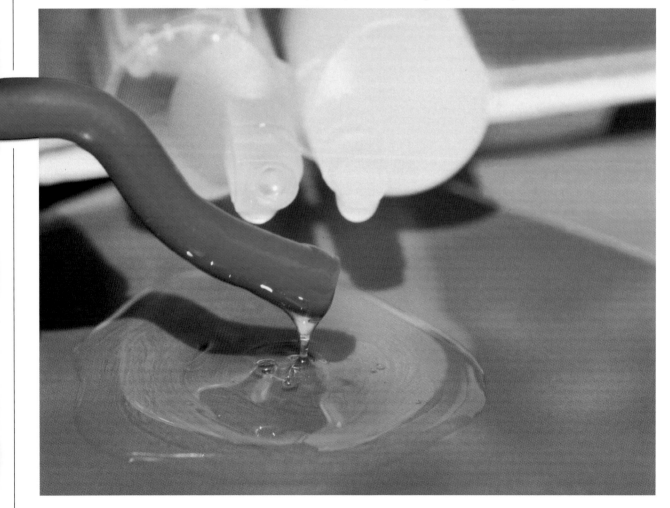

Epoxies (epoxy resins)

An epoxy resin is a polyether in which the plastic builds up in rings of three molecules. Epoxy resins were discovered by Americans J. MacIntosh and E.Y. Walford in 1920. In 1937 further progress was made by W.H. Moss in England in 1937, and from this came the first epoxy resin, trademarked Araldite®.

These structures easily bond with other substances and so are very good adhesives. They cure in air. Normally, epoxy resins are applied from two tubes, then mixed close to where they are to be used. They set hard quite quickly. Metal filler plastic is an example of an epoxy resin.

Epoxy resins can be used as solids. In this form they make the base of the printed circuit boards found in most electronic equipment.

Silicones

The name silicone comes from a discovery made in 1927 in England by Frederic Kipping. He named the substance "silicone" for what he thought was its structure, but it turned out that he was wrong, and the material is actually polysiloxane. However, the name remained.

Silicones, also called silicone rubbers, have alternating oxygen and silicon atoms in their backbones. They do not contain carbon and so are extremely unusual plastics. However, without the carbon they are also unreactive, resist water, and do not change with light or air.

Silicone is very flexible and can be forced through a tube into a long bead. That allows silicones to be used in a wide variety of ways, of which the most common home use is as a sealant around windows, shower trays, and baths.

See **Vol. 6: Dyes, paints, and adhesives** for more on epoxy resins.

(*Right*) Applying silicone rubber as a sealing strip. This material gives off a characteristic "acetic acid" smell as it cures.

(*Above*) Polyeurethane can be used for open-air seating.

Polyurethanes

Polyurethanes cover a wide range of plastics that have many common uses. They appear as a rubber substitute and are made into foams, fibers, and surface coatings.

Polyurethane is a unique material that offers the elasticity of rubber combined with the toughness and durability of metal. Because polyurethane is available in a very broad hardness range (eraser soft to bowling-ball hard), rubber, plastic, and metal can often be replaced with a material that resists abrasion, is lightweight, and is relatively cheap.

Polyurethane can be used for solid wheels on, among other things, skateboards, rollerskates, bowling balls, shock-absorbing pads around moving machines, and the soles of shoes.

Because polyurethane does not tear easily, it is a better material to use than rubber for belts that connect motors to machines. It is also used to replace

(*Right*) Skateboard wheels are often made from polyurethane.

metal for gears when they need to operate very quietly, for example, in the zoom lenses of video cameras. Polyurethane can also be flexed back and forth many times before it shows any signs of cracking. For this reason it is used as covers on, for example, gear sticks on machines. Polyurethane also has outstanding resistance to oxygen, ozone, sunlight, and general weather conditions.

Polyurethane foam was produced by accident in 1941 in Germany, when a trace of moisture reacted with the plastic to produce carbon dioxide gas, which then made the bubbles that foamed the plastic.

Polyurethane foam is used widely in upholstery. It makes many artificial sponges. It can be made both soft and rigid. Rigid foam is used for some kinds of packaging and for insulation.

Polyurethanes can be made into an elastic fiber that is commonly known under the trade name spandex. This fiber contains alternating rigid and flexible segments. Spandex is used for medical elastic bandages, swimwear, and sportswear.

(*Above*) Thermosets can be foamed and used for a variety of purposes, such as artificial flower supports or hole fillers.

Set Glossary

ACID RAIN: Rain that falls after having been contaminated by acid gases produced by power plants, vehicle exhausts, and other man-made sources.

ACIDITY: The tendency of a liquid to behave like an acid, reacting with metals and alkalis.

ADDITION POLYMERIZATION: The building blocks of many plastics (or polymers) are simple molecules called monomers. Monomers can be converted into polymers by making the monomers link to one another to form long chains in head-to-tail fashion. This is called addition polymerization or chain polymerization. It is most often used to link vinyl monomers to produce, for example, PVC, or polyvinyl chloride polymer.
See also **CONDENSATION POLYMERIZATION**

ADHESIVE: Any substance that can hold materials together simply by using some kind of surface attachment. In some cases this is a chemical reaction; in other cases it is a physical attraction between molecules of the adhesive and molecules of the substance it sticks to.

ADOBE: Simple unbaked brick made with mud, straw, and dung. It is dried in the open air. In this form it is very vulnerable to the effects of rainfall and so is most often found in desert areas or alternatively is protected by some waterproof covering, for example, thatch, straw, or reeds.

ALKALI: A base, or substance that can neutralize acids. In glassmaking an alkali is usually potassium carbonate and used as a flux to lower the melting point of the silica.

ALKYD: Any kind of synthetic resin used for protective coatings such as paint.

ALLOY: A metal mixture made up of two or more elements. Most of the elements used to make an alloy are metals. For example, brass is an alloy of copper and zinc, but carbon is an exception and used to make steel from iron.

AMALGAM: An alloy of mercury and one or more other metals. Dentist's filling amalgam traditionally contains mercury, silver, and tin.

AMPHIBIOUS: Adapted to function on both water and land.

AMORPHOUS: Shapeless and having no crystalline form. Glass is an amorphous solid.

ANION: An ion with a negative charge.

ANNEALING: A way of making a metal, alloy, or glass less brittle and more easy to work (more ductile) by heating it to a certain temperature (depending on the metal), holding it at that temperature for a certain time, and then cooling to room temperature.

ANODIZING: A method of plating metal by electrically depositing an oxide film onto the surface of a metal. The main purpose is to reduce corrosion.

ANTICYCLONE: A region of the Earth's atmosphere where the pressure is greater than average.

AQUEOUS SOLUTION: A substance dissolved in water.

ARTIFACT: An object of a previous time that was created by humans.

ARTIFICIAL DYE: A dye made from a chemical reaction that does not occur in nature. Dyes made from petroleum products are artificial dyes.

ARTIFICIAL FIBER: A fiber made from a material that has been manufactured, and that does not occur naturally. Rayon is an example of an artificial fiber.
Compare to **SYNTHETIC**

ATMOSPHERE: The envelope of gases that surrounds the Earth.

ATOM: The smallest particle of an element; a nucleus and its surrounding electrons.

AZO: A chemical compound that contains two nitrogen atoms joined by a double bond and each linked to a carbon atom. Azon compounds make up more than half of all dyes.

BARK: The exterior protective sheath of the stem and root of a woody plant such as a tree or a shrub. Everything beyond the cambium layer.

BAROMETER: An instrument for measuring atmospheric pressure.

BASE METAL: Having a low value and poorer properties than some other metals. Used, for example, when describing coins that contain metals other than gold or silver.

BAST FIBERS: A strong woody fiber that comes from the phloem of plants and is used for rope and similar products. Flax is an example of a bast fiber.

BATCH: A mixture of raw materials or products that are processes in a tank or kiln. This process produces small amounts of material or products and can be contrasted to continuous processes. Batch processing is used to make metals, alloys, glass, plastics, bricks, and other ceramics, dyes, and adhesives.

BAUXITE: A hydrated impure oxide of aluminum. It is the main ore used to obtain aluminum metal. The reddish-brown color of bauxite is caused by impurities of iron oxides.

BINDER: A substance used to make sure the pigment in a paint sticks to the surface it is applied to.

BIOCERAMICS: Ceramic materials that are used for medical and dental purposes, mainly as implants and replacements.

BLAST FURNACE: A tall furnace charged with a mixture of iron ore, coke, and limestone and used for the refining (smelting) of iron ore. The name comes from the strong blast of air used during smelting.

BLOWING: Forming a glass object by blowing into a gob of molten glass to form a bubble on the end of a blowpipe.

BOLL: The part of the cotton seed that contains the cotton fiber.

BOILING POINT: The temperature at which a liquid changes to a vapor. Boiling points change with atmospheric pressure.

BOND: A transfer or a sharing of electrons by two or more atoms. There are a number of kinds of chemical bonds, some very strong, such as covalent bonding and ionic bonding, and others quite weak, as in hydrogen bonding. Chemical bonds form because the linked molecules are more stable than the unlinked atoms from which they are formed.

BOYLE'S LAW: At constant temperature and for a given mass of gas the volume of the gas is inversely proportional to the pressure that builds up.

BRITTLE: Something that has almost no plasticity and so shatters rather than bends when a force is applied.

BULL'S EYE: A piece of glass with concentric rings marking the place where the blowpipe was attached to the glass. It is the central part of a pane of crown glass.

BUOYANCY: The tendency of an object to float if it is less dense than the liquid it is placed in.

BURN: A combustion reaction in which a flame is produced. A flame occurs where gases combust and release heat and light. At least two gases are therefore required if there is to be a flame.

CALORIFIC: Relating to the production of heat.

CAMBIUM: A thin growing layer that separates the xylem and phloem in most plants, and that produces new cell layers.

CAPACITOR: An electronic device designed for the temporary storage of electricity.

CAPILLARY ACTION, CAPILLARITY: The process by which surface tension forces can draw a liquid up a fine-bore tube.

CARBOHYDRATES: One of the main constituents of green plants, containing compounds of carbon, hydrogen, and oxygen. The main kinds of carbohydrate are sugars, starches, and celluloses.

CARBON COMPOUNDS: Any compound that includes the element carbon. Carbon compounds are also called organic compounds because they form an essential part of all living organisms.

CARBON CYCLE: The continuous movement of carbon between living things, the soil, the atmosphere, oceans, and rocks, especially those containing coal and petroleum.

CAST: To pour a liquid metal, glass, or other material into a mold and allow it to cool so that it solidifies and takes on the shape of the mold.

CATALYST: A substance that speeds up a chemical reaction but itself remains unchanged. For example, platinum is used in a catalytic converter of gases in the exhausts leaving motor vehicles.

CATALYTIC EFFECT: The way a substance helps speed up a reaction even though that substance does not form part of the reaction.

CATHODIC PROTECTION: The technique of protecting a metal object by connecting it to a more easily oxidizable material. The metal object being protected is made into the cathode of a cell. For example, iron can be protected by coupling it with magnesium.

CATION: An ion with a positive charge, often a metal.

CELL: A vessel containing two electrodes and a liquid substance that conducts electricity (an electrolyte).

CELLULOSE: A form of carbohydrate. *See* **CARBOHYDRATE**

CEMENT: A mixture of alumina, silica, lime, iron oxide, and magnesium oxide that is burned together in a kiln and then made into a powder. It is used as the main ingredient of mortar and as the adhesive in concrete.

CERAMIC: A crystalline nonmetal. In a more everyday sense it is a material based on clay that has been heated so that it has chemically hardened.

CHARRING: To burn partly so that some of a material turns to carbon and turns black.

CHINA: A shortened version of the original "Chinese porcelain," it also refers to various porcelain objects such as plates and vases meant for domestic use.

CHINA CLAY: The mineral kaolinite, which is a very white clay used as the basis of porcelain manufacture.

CLAY MINERALS: The minerals, such as kaolinite, illite, and montmorillonite, that occur naturally in soils and some rocks, and that are all minute platelike crystals.

COKE: A form of coal that has been roasted in the absence of air to remove much of the liquid and gas content.

COLORANTS: Any substance that adds a color to a material. The pigments in paints and the chemicals that make dyes are colorants.

COLORFAST: A dye that will not "run" in water or change color when it is exposed to sunlight.

COMPOSITE MATERIALS: Materials such as plywood that are normally regarded as a single material, but that themselves are made up of a number of different materials bonded together.

COMPOUND: A chemical consisting of two or more elements chemically bonded together, for example, calcium carbonate.

COMPRESSED AIR: Air that has been squashed to reduce its volume.

COMPRESSION: To be squashed.

COMPRESSION MOLDING: The shaping of an object, such as a headlight lens, which is achieved by squashing it into a mold.

CONCRETE: A mixture of cement and a coarse material such as sand and small stones.

CONDENSATION: The process of changing a gas to a liquid.

CONDENSATION POLYMERIZATION: The production of a polymer formed by a chain of reactions in which a water molecule is eliminated as every link of the polymer is formed. Polyester is an example.

CONDUCTION: (i) The exchange of heat (heat conduction) by contact with another object, or (ii) allowing the flow of electrons (electrical conduction).

CONDUCTIVITY: The property of allowing the flow of heat or electricity.

CONDUCTOR: (i) Heat—a material that allows heat to flow in and out of it easily. (ii) Electricity—a material that allows electrons to flow through it easily.

CONTACT ADHESIVE: An adhesive that, when placed on the surface to be joined, sticks as soon as the surfaces are placed firmly together.

CONVECTION: The circulating movement of molecules in a liquid or gas as a result of heating it from below.

CORRODE/CORROSION: A reaction usually between a metal and an acid or alkali in which the metal decomposes. The word is used in the sense of the metal being eaten away and dangerously thinned.

CORROSIVE: Causing corrosion, that is, the oxidation of a metal. For example, sodium hydroxide is corrosive.

COVALENT BONDING: The most common type of strong chemical bond, which occurs when two atoms share electrons. For example, oxygen O_2.

CRANKSHAFT: A rodlike piece of a machine designed to change linear into rotational motion or vice versa.

CRIMP: To cause to become wavy.

CRUCIBLE: A ceramic-lined container for holding molten metal, glass, and so on.

CRUDE OIL: A chemical mixture of petroleum liquids. Crude oil forms the raw material for an oil refinery.

CRYSTAL: A substance that has grown freely so that it can develop external faces.

CRYSTALLINE: A solid in which the atoms, ions, or molecules are organized into an orderly pattern without distinct crystal faces.

CURING: The process of allowing a chemical change to occur simply by waiting a while. Curing is often a process of reaction with water or with air.

CYLINDER GLASS: An old method of making window glass by blowing a large bubble of glass, then swinging it until it forms a cylinder. The ends of the cylinder are then cut off with shears and the sides of the cylinder allowed to open out until they form a flat sheet.

DECIDUOUS: A plant that sheds its leaves seasonally.

DECOMPOSE: To rot. Decomposing plant matter releases nutrients back to the soil and in this way provides nourishment for a new generation of living things.

DENSITY: The mass per unit volume (for example, g/c^3).

DESICCATE: To dry up thoroughly.

DETERGENT: A cleaning agent that is able to turn oils and dirts into an emulsion and then hold them in suspension so they can be washed away.

DIE: A tool for giving metal a required shape either by striking the object with the die or by forcing the object over or through the die.

DIFFUSION: The slow mixing of one substance with another until the two substances are evenly mixed. Mixing occurs because of differences in concentration within the mixture. Diffusion works rapidly with gases, very slowly with liquids.

DILUTE: To add more of a solvent to a solution.

DISSOCIATE: To break up. When a compound dissociates, its molecules break up into separate ions.

DISSOLVED: To break down a substance in a solution without causing a reaction.

DISTILLATION: The process of separating mixtures by condensing the vapors through cooling. The simplest form of distillation uses a Liebig condenser arranged with just a slight slope down to the collecting vessel. When the liquid mixture is heated and vapors are produced, they enter the water cooled condenser and then flow down the tube, where they can be collected.

DISTILLED WATER: Water that has its dissolved solids removed by the process of distillation.

DOPING: Adding an impurity to the surface of a substance in order to change its properties.

DORMANT: A period of inactivity such as during winter, when plants stop growing.

DRAWING: The process in which a piece of metal is pulled over a former or through dies.

DRY-CLEANED: A method of cleaning fabrics with nonwater-based organic solvents such as carbon tetrachloride.

DUCTILE: Capable of being drawn out or hammered thin.

DYE: A colored substance that will stick to another substance so that both appear to be colored.

EARLY WOOD: The wood growth put on the spring of each year.

EARTHENWARE: Pottery that has not been fired to the point where some of the clay crystals begin to melt and fuse together and is thus slightly porous and coarser than stoneware or porcelain.

ELASTIC: The ability of an object to regain its original shape after it has been deformed.

ELASTIC CHANGE: To change shape elastically.

ELASTICITY: The property of a substance that causes it to return to its original shape after it has been deformed in some way.

ELASTIC LIMIT: The largest force that a material can stand before it changes shape permanently.

ELECTRODE: A conductor that forms one terminal of a cell.

ELECTROLYSIS: An electrical-chemical process that uses an electric current to cause the breakup of a compound and the movement of metal ions in a solution. It is commonly used in industry for purifying (refining) metals or for plating metal objects with a fine, even metal coat.

ELECTROLYTE: An ionic solution that conducts electricity.

ELECTROMAGNET: A temporary magnet that is produced when a current of electricity passes through a coil of wire.

ELECTRON: A tiny, negatively charged particle that is part of an atom. The flow of electrons through a solid material such as a wire produces an electric current.

ELEMENT: A substance that cannot be decomposed into simpler substances by chemical means, for example, silver and copper.

EMULSION: Tiny droplets of one substance dispersed in another.

EMULSION PAINT: A paint made of an emulsion that is water soluble (also called latex paint).

ENAMEL: A substance made of finely powdered glass colored with a metallic oxide and suspended in oil so that it can be applied with a brush. The enamel is then heated, the oil burns away, and the glass fuses. Also used colloquially to refer to certain kinds of resin-based paint that have extremely durable properties.

ENGINEERED WOOD PRODUCTS: Wood products such as plywood sheeting made from a combination of wood sheets, chips or sawdust, and resin.

EVAPORATION: The change of state of a liquid to a gas. Evaporation happens below the boiling point.

EXOTHERMIC REACTION: A chemical reaction that gives out heat.

EXTRUSION: To push a substance through an opening so as to change its shape.

FABRIC: A material made by weaving threads into a network, often just referred to as cloth.

FELTED: Wool that has been hammered in the presence of heat and moisture to change its texture and mat the fibers.

FERRITE: A magnetic substance made of ferric oxide combined with manganese, nickel, or zinc oxide.

FIBER: A long thread.

FILAMENT: (i) The coiled wire used inside a light bulb. It consists of a high-resistance metal such as tungsten that also has a high melting point. (ii) A continuous thread produced during the manufacture of fibers.

FILLER: A material introduced in order to give bulk to a substance. Fillers are used in making paper and also in the manufacture of paints and some adhesives.

FILTRATE: The liquid that has passed through a filter.

FLOOD: When rivers spill over their banks and cover the surrounding land with water.

FLUID: Able to flow either as a liquid or a gas.

FLUORESCENT: A substance that gives out visible light when struck by invisible waves, such as ultraviolet rays.

FLUX: A substance that lowers the melting temperature of another substance. Fluxes are use in glassmaking and in melting alloys. A flux is used, for example, with a solder.

FORMER: An object used to control the shape or size of a product being made, for example, glass.

FOAM: A material that is sufficiently gelatinous to be able to contain bubbles of gas. The gas bulks up the substances, making it behave as though it were semirigid.

FORGE: To hammer a piece of heated metal until it changes to the desired shape.

FRACTION: A group of similar components of a mixture. In the petroleum industry the light fractions of crude oil are those with the smallest molecules, while the medium and heavy fractions have larger molecules.

FRACTIONAL DISTILLATION: The separation of the components of a liquid mixture by heating them to their boiling points.

FREEZING POINT: The temperature at which a substance undergoes a phase change from a liquid to a solid. It is the same temperature as the melting point.

FRIT: Partly fused materials of which glass is made.

FROTH SEPARATION: A process in which air bubbles are blown through a suspension, causing a froth of bubbles to collect on the surface. The materials that are attracted to the bubbles can then be removed with the froth.

FURNACE: An enclosed fire designed to produce a very high degree of heat for melting glass or metal or for reheating objects so they can be further processed.

FUSING: The process of melting particles of a material so they form a continuous sheet or solid object. Enamel is bonded to the surface of glass this way. Powder-formed metal is also fused into a solid piece. Powder paints are fused to the surface by heating.

GALVANIZING: The application of a surface coating of zinc to iron or steel.

GAS: A form of matter in which the molecules take no definite shape and are free to move around to uniformly fill any vessel they are put in. A gas can easily be compressed into a much smaller volume.

GIANT MOLECULES: Molecules that have been formed by polymerization.

GLASS: A homogeneous, often transparent material with a random noncrystalline molecular structure. It is achieved by cooling a molten substance very rapidly so that it cannot crystallize.

GLASS CERAMIC: A ceramic that is not entirely crystalline.

GLASSY STATE: A solid in which the molecules are arranged randomly rather than being formed into crystals.

GLOBAL WARMING: The progressive increase in the average temperature of the Earth's atmosphere, most probably in large part due to burning fossil fuels.

GLUE: An adhesive made from boiled animal bones.

GOB: A piece of near-molten glass used by glass-blowers and in machines to make hollow glass vessels.

GRAIN: (i) The distinctive pattern of fibers in wood. (ii) Small particles of a solid, including a single crystal.

GRAPHITE: A form of the element carbon with a sheetlike structure.

GRAVITY: The attractive force produced because of the mass of an object.

GREENHOUSE EFFECT: An increase in the global air temperature as a result of heat released from burning fossil fuels being absorbed by carbon dioxide in the atmosphere.

GREENHOUSE GAS: Any of various gases that contribute to the greenhouse effect, such as carbon dioxide.

GROUNDWATER: Water that flows naturally through rocks as part of the water cycle.

GUM: Any natural adhesive of plant origin that consists of colloidal polysaccharide substances that are gelatinous when moist but harden on drying.

HARDWOOD: The wood from a nonconiferous tree.

HEARTWOOD: The old, hard, nonliving central wood of trees.

HEAT: The energy that is transferred when a substance is at a different temperature than that of its surroundings.

HEAT CAPACITY: The ratio of the heat supplied to a substance compared with the rise in temperature that is produced.

HOLOGRAM: A three-dimensional image reproduced from a split laser beam.

HYDRATION: The process of absorption of water by a substance. In some cases hydration makes a substance change color, but in all cases there is a change in volume.

HYDROCARBON: A compound in which only hydrogen and carbon atoms are present. Most fuels are hydrocarbons, for example, methane.

HYDROFLUORIC ACID: An extremely corrosive acid that attacks silicate minerals such as glass. It is used to etch decoration onto glass and also to produce some forms of polished surface.

HYDROGEN BOND: A type of attractive force that holds one molecule to another. It is one of the weaker forms of intermolecular attractive force.

HYDROLYSIS: A reversible process of decomposition of a substance in water.

HYDROPHILIC: Attracted to water.

HYDROPHOBIC: Repelled by water.

IMMISCIBLE: Will not mix with another substance, for example, oil and water.

IMPURITIES: Any substances that are found in small quantities, and that are not meant to be in the solution or mixture.

INCANDESCENT: Glowing with heat, for example, a tungsten filament in a light bulb.

INDUSTRIAL REVOLUTION: The time, which began in the 18th century and continued through into the 19th century, when materials began to be made with the use of power machines and mass production.

INERT: A material that does not react chemically.

INORGANIC: A substance that does not contain the element carbon (and usually hydrogen), for example, sodium chloride.

INSOLUBLE: A substance that will not dissolve, for example, gold in water.

INSULATOR: A material that does not conduct electricity.

ION: An atom or group of atoms that has gained or lost one or more electrons and so developed an electrical charge.

IONIC BONDING: The form of bonding that occurs between two ions when the ions have opposite charges, for example, sodium ions bond with chloride ions to make sodium chloride. Ionic bonds are strong except in the presence of a solvent.

IONIZE: To change into ions.

ISOTOPE: An atom that has the same number of protons in its nucleus, but that has a different mass, for example, carbon 12 and carbon 14.

KAOLINITE: A form of clay mineral found concentrated as china clay. It is the result of the decomposition of the mineral feldspar.

KILN: An oven used to heat materials. Kilns at quite low temperatures are used to dry wood and at higher temperatures to bake bricks and to fuse enamel onto the surfaces of other substances. They are a form of furnace.

KINETIC ENERGY: The energy due to movement. When a ball is thrown, it has kinetic energy.

KNOT: The changed pattern in rings in wood due to the former presence of a branch.

LAMINATE: An engineered wood product consisting of several wood layers bonded by a resin. Also applies to strips of paper stuck together with resins to make such things as "formica" worktops.

LATE WOOD: Wood produced during the summer part of the growing season.

LATENT HEAT: The amount of heat that is absorbed or released during the process of changing state between gas, liquid, or solid. For example, heat is absorbed when liquid changes to gas. Heat is given out again as the gas condenses back to a liquid.

LATEX: A general term for a colloidal suspension of rubber-type material in water. Originally for the milky white liquid emulsion found in the Para rubber tree, but also now any manufactured water emulsion containing synthetic rubber or plastic.

LATEX PAINT: A water emulsion of a synthetic rubber or plastic used as paint. *See* **EMULSION PAINT**

LATHE: A tool consisting of a rotating spindle and cutters that is designed to produce shaped objects that are symmetrical about the axis of rotation.

LATTICE: A regular geometric arrangement of objects in space.

LEHR: The oven used for annealing glassware. It is usually a very long tunnel through which glass passes on a conveyor belt.

LIGHTFAST: A colorant that does not fade when exposed to sunlight.

LIGNIN: A form of hard cellulose that forms the walls of cells.

LIQUID: A form of matter that has a fixed volume but no fixed shape.

LUMBER: Timber that has been dressed for use in building or carpentry and consists of planed planks.

MALLEABLE: Capable of being hammered or rolled into a new shape without fracturing due to brittleness.

MANOMETER: A device for measuring liquid or gas pressure.

MASS: The amount of matter in an object. In common use the word weight is used instead (incorrectly) to mean mass.

MATERIAL: Anything made of matter.

MATTED: Another word for felted. *See* **FELTED**

MATTER: Anything that has mass and takes up space.

MELT: The liquid glass produced when a batch of raw materials melts. Also used to describe molten metal.

MELTING POINT: The temperature at which a substance changes state from a solid phase to a liquid phase. It is the same as the freezing point.

METAL: A class of elements that is a good conductor of electricity and heat, has a metallic luster, is malleable and ductile, and is formed as cations held together by a sea of electrons. A metal may also be an alloy of these elements and carbon.

METAL FATIGUE: The gradual weakening of a metal by constant bending until a crack develops.

MINERAL: A solid substance made of just one element or compound, for example, calcite minerals contain only calcium carbonate.

MISCIBLE: Capable of being mixed.

MIXTURE: A material that can be separated into two or more substances using physical means, for example, air.

MOLD: A containing shape made of wood, metal, or sand into which molten glass or metal is poured. In metalworking it produces a casting. In glassmaking the glass is often blown rather than poured when making, for example, light bulbs.

MOLECULE: A group of two or more atoms held together by chemical bonds.

MONOMER: A small molecule and building block for larger chain molecules or polymers (mono means "one" and mer means "part").

MORDANT: A chemical that is attracted to a dye and also to the surface that is to be dyed.

MOSAIC: A decorated surface made from a large number of small colored pieces of glass, natural stone, or ceramic that are cemented together.

NATIVE METAL: A pure form of a metal not combined as a compound. Native metals are more common in nonreactive elements such as gold than reactive ones such as calcium.

NATURAL DYES: Dyes made from plants without any chemical alteration, for example, indigo.

NATURAL FIBERS: Fibers obtained from plants or animals, for example, flax and wool.

NEUTRON: A particle inside the nucleus of an atom that is neutral and has no charge.

NOBLE GASES: The members of group 8 of the periodic table of the elements: helium, neon, argon, krypton, xenon, radon. These gases are almost entirely unreactive.

NONMETAL: A brittle substance that does not conduct electricity, for example, sulfur or nitrogen.

OIL-BASED PAINTS: Paints that are not based on water as a vehicle. Traditional artists' oil paint uses linseed oil as a vehicle.

OPAQUE: A substance through which light cannot pass.

ORE: A rock containing enough of a useful substance to make mining it worthwhile, for example, bauxite, the ore of aluminum.

ORGANIC: A substance that contains carbon and usually hydrogen. The carbonates are usually excluded.

OXIDE: A compound that includes oxygen and one other element, for example, Cu_2O, copper oxide.

OXIDIZE, OXIDIZING AGENT: A reaction that occurs when a substance combines with oxygen or a reaction in which an atom, ion, or molecule loses electrons to another substance (and in this more general case does not have to take up oxygen).

OZONE: A form of oxygen whose molecules contain three atoms of oxygen. Ozone high in the atmosphere blocks harmful ultraviolet rays from the Sun, but at ground level it is an irritant gas when breathed in and so is regarded as a form of pollution. The ozone layer is the uppermost part of the stratosphere.

PAINT: A coating that has both decorative and protective properties, and that consists of a pigment suspended in a vehicle, or binder, made of a resin dissolved in a solvent. It dries to give a tough film.

PARTIAL PRESSURE: The pressure a gas in a mixture would exert if it alone occupied the flask. For example, oxygen makes up about a fifth of the atmosphere. Its partial pressure is therefore about a fifth of normal atmospheric pressure.

PASTE: A thick suspension of a solid in a liquid.

PATINA: A surface coating that develops on metals and protects them from further corrosion, for example, the green coating of copper carbonate that forms on copper statues.

PERIODIC TABLE: A chart organizing elements by atomic number and chemical properties into groups and periods.

PERMANENT HARDNESS: Hardness in the water that cannot be removed by boiling.

PETROCHEMICAL: Any of a large group of manufactured chemicals (not fuels) that come from petroleum and natural gas. It is usually taken to include similar products that can be made from coal and plants.

PETROLEUM: A natural mixture of a range of gases, liquids, and solids derived from the decomposed remains of animals and plants.

PHASE: A particular state of matter. A substance can exist as a solid, liquid, or gas and may change between these phases with the addition or removal of energy, usually in the form of heat.

PHOSPHOR: A material that glows when energized by ultraviolet or electron beams, such as in fluorescent tubes and cathode ray tubes.

PHOTOCHEMICAL SMOG: A mixture of tiny particles of dust and soot combined with a brown haze caused by the reaction of colorless nitric oxide from vehicle exhausts and oxygen of the air to form brown nitrogen dioxide.

PHOTOCHROMIC GLASSES: Glasses designed to change color with the intensity of light. They use the property that certain substances, for example, silver halide, can change color (and change chemically) in light. For example, when silver chromide is dispersed in the glass melt, sunlight decomposes the silver halide to release silver (and so darken the lens). But the halogen cannot escape; and when the light is removed, the halogen recombines with the silver to turn back to colorless silver halide.

PHOTOSYNTHESIS: The natural process that happens in green plants whereby the energy from light is used to help turn gases, water, and minerals into tissue and energy.

PIEZOELECTRICS: Materials that produce electric currents when they are deformed, or vice versa.

PIGMENT: Insoluble particles of coloring material.

PITH: The central strand of spongy tissue found in the stems of most plants.

PLASTIC: Material—a carbon-based substance consisting of long chains or networks (polymers) of simple molecules. The word plastic is commonly used only for synthetic polymers. Property—a material is plastic if it can be made to change shape easily and then remain in this new shape (contrast with elasticity and brittleness).

PLASTIC CHANGE: A permanent change in shape that happens without breaking.

PLASTICIZER: A chemical added to rubbers and resins to make it easier for them to be deformed and molded. Plasticizers are also added to cement to make it more easily worked when used as a mortar.

PLATE GLASS: Rolled, ground, and polished sheet glass.

PLIABLE: Supple enough to be repeatedly bent without fracturing.

PLYWOOD: An engineered wood laminate consisting of sheets of wood bonded with resin. Each sheet of wood has the grain at right angles to the one above and below. This imparts stability to the product.

PNEUMATIC DEVICE: Any device that works with air pressure.

POLAR: Something that has a partial electric charge.

POLYAMIDES: A compound that contains more than one amide group, for example, nylon.

POLYMER: A compound that is made of long chains or branching networks by combining molecules called monomers as repeating units. Poly means "many," mer means "part."

PORCELAIN: A hard, fine-grained, and translucent white ceramic that is made of china clay and is fired to a high temperature. Varieties include china.

PORES: Spaces between particles that are small enough to hold water by capillary action, but large enough to allow water to enter.

POROUS: A material that has small cavities in it, known as pores. These pores may or may not be joined. As a result, porous materials may or may not allow a liquid or gas to pass through them. Popularly, porous is used to mean permeable, the kind of porosity in which the pores are joined, and liquids or gases can flow.

POROUS CERAMICS: Ceramics that have not been fired at temperatures high enough to cause the clays to fuse and so prevent the slow movement of water.

POTENTIAL ENERGY: Energy due to the position of an object. Water in a reservoir has potential energy because it is stored up, and when released, it moves down to a lower level.

POWDER COATING: The application of a pigment in powder form without the use of a solvent.

POWDER FORMING: A process of using a powder to fill a mold and then heating the powder to make it fuse into a solid.

PRECIPITATE: A solid substance formed as a result of a chemical reaction between two liquids or gases.

PRESSURE: The force per unit area measured in SI units in Pascals and also more generally in atmospheres.

PRIMARY COLORS: A set of colors from which all others can be made. In transmitted light they are red, blue, and green.

PROTEIN: Substances in plants and animals that include nitrogen.

PROTON: A positively charged particle in the nucleus of an atom that balances out the charge of the surrounding electrons.

QUENCH: To put into water in order to cool rapidly.

RADIATION: The transmission of energy from one body to another without any contribution from the intervening space. *Contrast with* **CONVECTION** and **CONDUCTION**

RADIOACTIVE: A substance that spontaneously emits energetic particles.

RARE EARTHS: Any of a group of metal oxides that are found widely throughout the Earth's rocks, but in low concentrations. They are mainly made up of the elements of the lanthanide series of the periodic table of the elements.

RAW MATERIAL: A substance that has not been prepared, but that has an intended use in manufacturing.

RAY: Narrow beam of light.

RAYON: An artificial fiber made from natural cellulose.

REACTION (CHEMICAL): The recombination of two substances using parts of each substance.

REACTIVE: A substance that easily reacts with many other substances.

RECYCLE: To take once used materials and make them available for reuse.

REDUCTION, REDUCING AGENT: The removal of oxygen from or the addition of hydrogen to a compound.

REFINING: Separating a mixture into the simpler substances of which it is made, especially petrochemical refining.

REFRACTION: The bending of a ray of light as it passes between substances of different refractive index (light-bending properties).

REFRACTORY: Relating to the use of a ceramic material, especially a brick, in high-temperature conditions of, for example, a furnace.

REFRIGERANT: A substance that, on changing between a liquid and a gas, can absorb large amounts of (latent) heat from its surroundings.

REGENERATED FIBERS: Fibers that have been dissolved in a solution and then recovered from the solution in a different form.

REINFORCED FIBER: A fiber that is mixed with a resin, for example, glass-reinforced fiber.

RESIN: A semisolid natural material that is made of plant secretions and often yellow-brown in color. Also synthetic materials with the same type of properties. Synthetic resins have taken over almost completely from natural resins and are available as thermoplastic resins and thermosetting resins.

RESPIRATION: The process of taking in oxygen and releasing carbon dioxide in animals and the reverse in plants.

RIVET: A small rod of metal that is inserted into two holes in metal sheets and then burred over at both ends in order to stick the sheets together.

ROCK: A naturally hard inorganic material composed of mineral particles or crystals.

ROLLING: The process in which metal is rolled into plates and bars.

ROSIN: A brittle form of resin used in varnishes.

RUST: The product of the corrosion of iron and steel in the presence of air and water.

SALT: Generally thought of as sodium chloride, common salt; however, more generally a salt is a compound involving a metal. There are therefore many "salts" in water in addition to sodium chloride.

SAPWOOD: The outer, living layers of the tree, which includes cells for the transportation of water and minerals between roots and leaves.

SATURATED: A state in which a liquid can hold no more of a substance dissolved in it.

SEALANTS: A material designed to stop water or other liquids from penetrating into a surface or between surfaces. Most sealants are adhesives.

SEMICONDUCTOR: A crystalline solid that has an electrical conductivity part way between a conductor and an insulator. This material can be altered by doping to control an electric current. Semiconductors are the basis of transistors, integrated circuits, and other modern electronic solid-state devices.

SEMIPERMEABLE MEMBRANE: A thin material that acts as a fine sieve or filter, allowing small molecules to pass, but holding back large molecules.

SEPARATING COLUMN: A tall glass tube containing a porous disk near the base and filled with a substance such as aluminum oxide that can absorb materials on its surface. When a mixture passes through the columns, fractions are retarded by differing amounts so that each fraction is washed through the column in sequence.

SEPARATING FUNNEL: A pear-shaped glass funnel designed to permit the separation of immiscible liquids by simply pouring off the more dense liquid from the bottom of the funnel, while leaving the less dense liquid in the funnel.

SHAKES: A defect in wood produced by the wood tissue separating, usually parallel to the rings.

SHEEN: A lustrous, shiny surface on a yarn. It is produced by the finishing process or may be a natural part of the yarn.

SHEET-METAL FORMING: The process of rolling out metal into sheet.

SILICA: Silicon dioxide, most commonly in the form of sand.

SILICA GLASS: Glass made exclusively of silica.

SINTER: The process of heating that makes grains of a ceramic or metal a solid mass before it becomes molten.

SIZE: A glue, varnish, resin, or similar very dilute adhesive sealant used to block up the pores in porous surfaces or, for example, plaster and paper. Once the size has dried, paint or other surface coatings can be applied without the coating sinking in.

SLAG: A mixture of substances that are waste products of a furnace. Most slag are mainly composed of silicates.

SMELTING: Roasting a substance in order to extract the metal contained in it.

SODA: A flux for glassmaking consisting of sodium carbonate.

SOFTWOOD: Wood obtained from a coniferous tree.

SOLID: A rigid form of matter that maintains its shape regardless of whether or not it is in a container.

SOLIDIFICATION: Changing from a liquid to a solid.

SOLUBILITY: The maximum amount of a substance that can be contained in a solvent.

SOLUBLE: Readily dissolvable in a solvent.

SOLUTION: A mixture of a liquid (the solvent) and at least one other substance of lesser abundance (the solute). Like all mixtures, solutions can be separated by physical means.

SOLVAY PROCESS: Modern method of manufacturing the industrial alkali sodium carbonate (soda ash).

SOLVENT: The main substance in a solution.

SPECTRUM: A progressive series arranged in order, for example, the range of colors that make up visible light as seen in a rainbow.

SPINNERET: A small metal nozzle perforated with many small holes through which a filament solution is forced. The filaments that emerge are solidified by cooling and the filaments twisted together to form a yarn.

SPINNING: The process of drawing out and twisting short fibers, for example, wool, and thus making a thread or yarn.

SPRING: A natural flow of water from the ground.

STABILIZER: A chemical that, when added to other chemicals, prevents further reactions. For example, in soda lime glass the lime acts as a stabilizer for the silica.

STAPLE: A short fiber that has to be twisted with other fibers (spun) in order to make a long thread or yarn.

STARCHES: One form of carbohydrate. Starches can be used to make adhesives.

STATE OF MATTER: The physical form of matter. There are three states of matter: liquid, solid, and gas.

STEAM: Water vapor at the boiling point of water.

STONEWARE: Nonwhite pottery that has been fired at a high temperature until some of the clay has fused, a state called vitrified. Vitrification makes the pottery impervious to water. It is used for general tableware, often for breakfast crockery.

STRAND: When a number of yarns are twisted together, they make a strand. Strands twisted together make a rope.

SUBSTANCE: A type of material including mixtures.

SULFIDE: A compound that is composed only of metal and sulfur atoms, for example, PbS, the mineral galena.

SUPERCONDUCTORS: Materials that will conduct electricity with virtually no resistance if they are cooled to temperatures close to absolute zero (–273°C).

SURFACE TENSION: The force that operates on the surface of a liquid, and that makes it act as though it were covered with an invisible elastic film.

SURFACTANT: A substance that acts on a surface, such as a detergent.

SUSPENDED, SUSPENSION: Tiny particles in a liquid or a gas that do not settle out with time.

SYNTHETIC: Something that does not occur naturally but has to be manufactured. Synthetics are often produced from materials that do not occur in nature, for example, from petrochemicals. (i) Dye—a synthetic dye is made from petrochemicals, as opposed to natural dyes that are made of extracts of plants. (ii) Fiber—synthetic is a subdivision of artificial. Although both polyester and rayon are artificial fibers, rayon is made from reconstituted natural cellulose fibers and so is not synthetic, while polyester is made from petrochemicals and so is a synthetic fiber.

TANNIN: A group of pale-yellow or light-brown substances derived from plants that are used in dyeing fabric and making ink. Tannins are soluble in water and produce dark-blue or dark-green solutions when added to iron compounds.

TARNISH: A coating that develops as a result of the reaction between a metal and the substances in the air. The most common form of tarnishing is a very thin transparent oxide coating, such as occurs on aluminum. Sulfur compounds in the air make silver tarnish black.

TEMPER: To moderate or to make stronger: used in the metal industry to describe softening hardened steel or cast iron by reheating at a lower temperature or to describe hardening steel by reheating and cooling in oil; or in the glass industry, to describe toughening glass by first heating it and then slowly cooling it.

TEMPORARILY HARD WATER: Hard water that contains dissolved substances that can be removed by boiling.

TENSILE (PULLING STRENGTH): The greatest lengthwise (pulling) stress a substance can bear without tearing apart.

TENSION: A state of being pulled. Compare to compression.

TERRA COTTA: Red earth-colored glazed or unglazed fired clay whose origins lie in the Mediterranean region of Europe.

THERMOPLASTIC: A plastic that will soften and can be molded repeatedly into different shapes. It will then set into the molded shape as it cools.

THERMOSET: A plastic that will set into a molded shape as it first cools, but that cannot be made soft again by reheating.

THREAD: A long length of filament, group of filaments twisted together, or a long length of short fibers that have been spun and twisted together into a continuous strand.

TIMBER: A general term for wood suitable for building or for carpentry and consisting of roughcut planks. *Compare to* LUMBER

TRANSITION METALS: Any of the group of metallic elements (for example, chromium and iron) that belong to the central part of the periodic table of the elements and whose oxides commonly occur in a variety of colors.

TRANSPARENT: Something that will readily let light through, for example, window glass. Compare to translucent, when only some light gets through but an image cannot be seen, for example, greaseproof paper.

TROPOSPHERE: The lower part of the atmosphere in which clouds form. In general, temperature decreases with height.

TRUNK: The main stem of a tree.

VACUUM: Something from which all air has been removed.

VAPOR: The gaseous phase of a substance that is a liquid or a solid at that temperature, for example, water vapor is the gaseous form of water.

VAPORIZE: To change from a liquid to a gas, or vapor.

VENEER: A thin sheet of highly decorative wood that is applied to cheap wood or engineered wood products to improve their appearance and value.

VINYL: Often used as a general name for plastic. Strictly, vinyls are polymers derived from ethylene by removal of one hydrogen atom, for example, PVC, polyvinylchloride.

VISCOSE: A yellow-brown solution made by treating cellulose with alkali solution and carbon disulfide and used to make rayon.

VISCOUS, VISCOSITY: Sticky. Viscosity is a measure of the resistance of a liquid to flow. The higher the viscosity—the more viscous it is—the less easily it will flow.

VITREOUS CHINA: A translucent form of china or porcelain.

VITRIFICATION: To heat until a substance changes into a glassy form and fuses together.

VOLATILE: Readily forms a gas. Some parts of a liquid mixture are often volatile, as is the case for crude oil. This allows them to be separated by distillation.

WATER CYCLE: The continual interchange of water between the oceans, the air, clouds, rain, rivers, ice sheets, soil, and rocks.

WATER VAPOR: The gaseous form of water.

WAVELENGTH: The distance between adjacent crests on a wave. Shorter wavelengths have smaller distances between crests than longer wavelengths.

WAX: Substances of animal, plant, mineral, or synthetic origin that are similar to fats but are less greasy and harder. They form hard films that can be polished.

WEAVING: A way of making a fabric by passing two sets of yarns through one another at right angles to make a kind of tight meshed net with no spaces between the yarns.

WELDING: Technique used for joining metal pieces through intense localized heat. Welding often involves the use of a joining metal such as a rod of steel used to attach steel pieces (arc welding).

WETTING: In adhesive spreading, a term that refers to the complete coverage of an adhesive over a surface.

WETTING AGENT: A substance that is able to cover a surface completely with a film of liquid. It is a substance with a very low surface tension.

WHITE GLASS: Also known as milk glass, it is an opaque white glass that was originally made in Venice and meant to look like porcelain.

WROUGHT IRON: A form of iron that is relatively soft and can be bent without breaking. It contains less than 0.1% carbon.

YARN: A strand of fibers twisted together and used to make textiles.

Set Index

USING THE SET INDEX

This index covers all nine volumes in the *Materials Science* set:

Volume number	Title
1:	Plastics
2:	Metals
3:	Wood and paper
4:	Ceramics
5:	Glass
6:	Dyes, paints, and adhesives
7:	Fibers
8:	Water
9:	Air

An example entry:

Index entries are listed alphabetically.

sinter, sintering **2:** 21; **4:** 9, 44

Volume numbers are in bold and are followed by page references.

In the example above, "sinter, sintering" appears in Volume 2: Metals on page 21 and in Volume 4: Ceramics on pages 9 and 44. Many terms also are covered in the Glossary on pages 58–64.

See or *see also* refers to another entry where there will be additional relevant information.

A

abrasive **4:** 6, 12
ABS. *See* acrylonitrile-butadiene-styrene
acetate fiber **6:** 21; **7:** 36, 46
acetate film **1:** 47
acetic acid **1:** 37, 55
acid rain **8:** 57; **9:** 21, 46, 47
acidic water **8:** 6, 7, 46, 48, 52, 57
acids **1:** 15; **2:** 28, 30; **8:** 6, 46, 47, 48, 52, 56, 57
acrylic **1:** 38, 39, 40, 41
acrylic adhesives **6:** 50
acrylic fiber **1:** 39; **6:** 20, 21; **7:** 33, 36, 37, 38, 44, 45, 57
acrylic paints and stains **1:** 41; **6:** 32, 34, 35
acrylic plastics **1:** 38-41
acrylic powders **6:** 40
acrylonitrile-butadiene-styrene (ABS) **1:** 38
addition polymers/addition polymerization **1:** 10, 11, 27, 43; **7:** 15
additives **1:** 15, 16, 17; **3:** 51
adhesion **6:** 44, 45, 46
adhesives **1:** 22, 37, 40, 41, 42, 44, 53, 55; **3:** 8, 24, 43, 44, 45, 47, 50, 53, 54; **4:** 35, 41; **5:** 54; **6:** 4, 41-57

adhesive tapes **6:** 54, 57
admiralty brass **2:** 24
adobe **4:** 10, 11
advanced ceramics **4:** 42-57
aggregate **4:** 39, 41
air **9:** 4 AND THROUGHOUT
air bags **9:** 42
air brakes **9:** 35
air conditioning **9:** 26, 52
aircraft **2:** 21, 26, 27, 35, 51; **9:** 29, 32, 34, 35
air cushions **9:** 34-35
air drying **3:** 36
air gun **9:** 35
air in transportation **9:** 32
air pollution **9:** 19, 38-40, 44, 46-47
air pressure **9:** 5, 6, 28, 32, 37
albumen **6:** 49
alcohols **8:** 45, 51
alizarin **6:** 12, 13, 14
alkalis **1:** 15; **2:** 28, 30; **8:** 52
alkyd-based paint **6:** 31, 33
alkyd-based varnishes **6:** 37
alloys, alloying **1:** 15; **2:** 6, 13, 22, 23-27, 28, 34, 35, 37, 42; **4:** 46
alum **3:** 53; **6:** 10
alumina **4:** 38, 46, 50, 51, 54, 56, 57; **5:** 8, 9, 10, 13, 18, 52
aluminosilicates **4:** 14
aluminum **2:** 4, 5, 9, 10, 18, 19, 20, 21, 23, 24, 26, 27, 29, 30, 32, 50, 53; **4:** 14, 36
aluminum oxide **4:** 46, 50, 57; **5:** 13
amalgams **4:** 55
amides **7:** 10, 47
ammonia **9:** 41
amorphous solid **5:** 5, 15
amphibious vehicles **9:** 33
anaerobics **6:** 50
ancient glass **5:** 29
angle of incidence **5:** 20
aniline dyes **6:** 14, 22; **7:** 38
aniline mauve **6:** 14
animal glue **6:** 49
anions **8:** 10
annealing **5:** 50
anodized duralumin **2:** 32
anodizing **2:** 27, 32
antimony **2:** 45
antirust paint **6:** 33
anvil **2:** 12, 20
aqueous solutions **8:** 43, 44, 46
Araldite® **1:** 55
aramids **7:** 36, 50, 51
Archimedes' principle **8:** 38
argon **9:** 18, 36, 54, 55
armor **2:** 42, 43
armor plating **2:** 42
Arnel® **1:** 47; **7:** 46
arsenic oxide **5:** 11
artifacts **4:** 12
artificial dyes **6:** 7
artificial fibers **3:** 50; **7:** 7, 8, 9, 10, 12, 15, 16, 17, 19, 24, 30, 31, 32-57
artificial polymers **7:** 12
aspen **3:** 15
atmosphere **9:** 12, 14, 18, 20-21, 43, 44, 54, 55
atmospheric pressure **8:** 21, 22, 28; **9:** 6. *See also* air pressure
atomizer **9:** 28

atoms **2:** 6, 8, 9, 22, 23; **4:** 5, 9; **5:** 4, 5, 39; **7:** 4, 9; **8:** 8; **9:** 8, 10
atoms, properties in plastics **1:** 13
ax **3:** 6
azo dyes and pigments **6:** 7, 10; **7:** 38

B

backbone chain **1:** 27, 43, 55; **7:** 4. *See also* polymers
backbone unit **1:** 54. *See also* monomers
bagasse **3:** 49
Bakelite **1:** 43
balloons **9:** 8, 14, 51, 54
balsa **3:** 17, 20, 23
bamboo **3:** 49
band saw **3:** 34
barbed wire **2:** 6, 30, 31
barium carbonate **4:** 46; **5:** 9
barium titanate **4:** 46
bark **3:** 4, 6, 13, 14, 32
barometer **8:** 28
base metal **2:** 23, 24
bast fibers **7:** 20
batch kiln **4:** 19, 28
batch processing **7:** 32
batik **6:** 19
bauxite **4:** 38
beating metals **2:** 22-23
beech **3:** 17, 18, 23
bellows **9:** 28
bells **2:** 14, 44
bending ceramics **4:** 9
bending metals **2:** 12, 22, 35, 51
bends, the **9:** 42
benzene **1:** 33, 39
benzene ring **1:** 10; **6:** 15
Bessemer converter **2:** 46
Bessemer, Henry **2:** 47
binder **4:** 55; **6:** 27, 39
bioceramics **4:** 54-56
blacksmith **2:** 12, 22, 41
blast furnace **2:** 47
bleaches **6:** 24, 26
bleaching paper **3:** 52, 57
blending fibers **7:** 12, 25, 41, 43, 44, 45
blends, blending ceramics **4:** 17, 22, 36, 38
blood **8:** 6, 48
blood glue **6:** 49
bloom **2:** 40
blow molding **1:** 19
blown glass **5:** 32-33
board **3:** 34, 36, 42, 43, 44, 45, 46
bobbin **7:** 25, 42
boil, boiling water **8:** 11, 16, 20, 48
boilers **8:** 21, 22, 32, 33, 54
boiling point of water 11, 19, 20, 49, 48, 54
boll, boll fiber **7:** 4, 20, 25
bond paper **3:** 55
bonds and bonding **2:** 6, 7; **4:** 4, 5, 6, 9, 15, 25; **8:** 8, 9, 11, 14. *See also* covalent bonding, hydrogen bonds and bonding, ionic bonding
bone china **4:** 25
book paper **3:** 55
borax **5:** 13
boric oxide **5:** 8, 13
borosilicate glass **5:** 12, 13, 19
bottles **5:** 10, 28, 30, 43, 46-47
Boyle's law **9:** 8, 9
brass **2:** 6, 16, 24, 34, 41, 44

brazilwood **6:** 12
brick **8:** 26, 27, 28
brick colors **4:** 15, 16, 27, 29
bricks and brick making **4:** 4, 10, 14, 15, 16, 17, 19, 26-31, 32, 33, 34, 39
brighteners, for fabric and paper **6:** 24
brine **8:** 41, 47, 50, 51
bristles **7:** 6, 48
brittleness in materials **2:** 4, 8, 14, 17, 18, 41; **3:** 19; **4:** 4, 8-9; **5:** 5, 23
broad-leaved trees **3:** 17
bronze **2:** 15, 25, 37, 38, 39, 40, 41, 43, 44, 45, 55
Bronze Age **2:** 14, 37-38, 40, 41, 55
buildings, use of metals in **2:** 18, 28, 31, 49, 54-57
bull's-eye glass **5:** 39
bulletproof glass **5:** 26
bulletproof vests **7:** 8, 14, 34, 51
bullets **2:** 42, 45
buoyancy **8:** 38-39
burlap **7:** 11
burn **3:** 27, 28
burning plastics **1:** 12, 13, 14, 25
butadiene rubber **1:** 42
butene **1:** 28

C
cadmium **2:** 10, 30
calcium **2:** 5, 10; **4:** 15, 36, 53
calcium halophosphate **4:** 52
calcium oxide **4:** 37, 38; **5:** 8
calcium silicate **4:** 52
calcium sulfate **4:** 34
calcium tungstate **4:** 52
calorific value of wood **3:** 28
cambium **3:** 10, 12, 13, 14
cannons **2:** 15, 25, 44, 45
canoes **1:** 53; **3:** 6
canvas **7:** 11
capacitors **4:** 7, 44, 46-47; **5:** 18
capillarity **8:** 26-28
capillary action **6:** 54
car industry **2:** 49, 52
carbohydrates **7:** 10
carbon **1:** 4, 6, 7, 10, 13, 16, 27, 28, 39, 41, 42, 43, 54, 55, 57; **2:** 10, 23, 39, 41; **4:** 6; **7:** 4, 7, 8, 14, 49, 50, 53, 55, 56; **9:** 21, 48, 49
carbon black **1:** 42; **6:** 9, 29
carbon chains **1:** 7, 13, 27
carbon compounds **1:** 4; **6:** 9
carbon cycle **9:** 48, 49
carbon dioxide **9:** 11, 19, 36, 43, 48-50, 51
carbon fiber **4:** 57; **7:** 56-57
carbonic acid **8:** 48
cardboard **3:** 46, 56
carding **7:** 25
carmine **6:** 12, 13, 14
carpets **7:** 24, 25, 27, 33, 43, 44, 45, 48, 49
carving **3:** 9, 22
casein **6:** 49
cashmere **7:** 27
cassiterite **2:** 38
cast bronze **2:** 15, 45
cast glass **5:** 30
casting **2:** 13, 14-17, 18, 25, 38, 39, 44; **4:** 17, 18, 43
cast iron **2:** 40, 41, 45, 49, 54, 55, 56, 57
catalysts **7:** 15, 42; **8:** 7; **9:** 10, 41

catalytic converters **2:** 11; **4:** 43, 53, 57; **9:** 39, 40
cations **4:** 6, 15; **8:** 10
cedar **3:** 16
Celanese® **7:** 46
cellophane **1:** 47
cells **3:** 10-3, 14, 18, 22, 23, 27, 28
celluloid **1:** 7, 46
cellulose **1:** 44, 46, 47, 49; **3:** 10, 46, 47, 48, 50, 51, 52; **7:** 10, 11, 12, 13, 25, 31, 39, 40, 41, 46
cellulose diacetate **1:** 47
cement **4:** 10, 13, 35-37, 38, 39, 40, 41. *See also* dental cement
central heating systems **2:** 56; **8:** 32, 33; **9:** 25, 26, 27
ceramic **4:** 4 AND THROUGHOUT
ceramic capacitors **4:** 46-47
ceramic electrical insulators **3:** 28; **9:** 22
ceramic molds **1:** 9
ceramics **1:** 15, 16; **2:** 4, 12, 49; **5:** 4, 5, 14
ceramics used in nuclear reactors **4:** 54
ceramic tiles. *See* tiles
CFCs. *See* chlorofluorocarbons
chain mail **2:** 42
chalcogenide glasses **5:** 15
change of state **8:** 5, 16-20, 21, 22; **9:** 52
charcoal **2:** 38, 39, 40, 41, 46, 47
Charles's law **9:** 9
charring **7:** 7, 10, 15, 17, 24, 33, 39, 44, 57
checks **3:** 20
chemical properties of glass **5:** 16-18
chewing gum **1:** 8
chicle **1:** 8
china **4:** 25
china clay **3:** 51, 54; **4:** 14, 16, 24, 25; **6:** 9
chipboard, chipwood **1:** 22; **3:** 34, 42, 43, 44
chips, chippings **3:** 11, 32, 34, 50
chlorine **1:** 10, 29, 39; **3:** 52
chloroethylene **1:** 10
chlorofluorocarbons (CFCs) **9:** 44
chromium **2:** 10, 25, 28, 30; **5:** 11, 21
chromium plating **2:** 30, 34
circular saw **3:** 34
clay minerals **4:** 14
clays **4:** 4, 9, 10, 14, 15, 17, 18, 28
clay suspensions **4:** 17, 18
clearcut tree felling **3:** 32
cling wrap **1:** 11
clothing **7:** 8, 16, 29, 33, 39, 41, 43, 44, 45
clouds and cloud formation **8:** 4, 7; **9:** 3, 9, 20, 52, 53
coal **2:** 47, 49; **9:** 48, 49
coal tar **6:** 7, 8, 10, 16
coated papers **3:** 55
cobalt **2:** 9; **5:** 11, 21
cobalt aluminate **4:** 51
cobalt oxide **5:** 11
cobalt silicate **4:** 51
cochineal **6:** 12, 13
coins **2:** 20, 26, 38, 39
coir **7:** 11
coke **2:** 47
cold bending **2:** 35
cold forging **2:** 20, 23
cold rolling **2:** 18
cold-working metals **2:** 14
collecting gases **9:** 10
colorants **1:** 15, 16; **6:** 6, 9, 10, 24, 25, 26

colored glass **5:** 21, 33-35
colorfast **6:** 8; **7:** 52
coloring glass **5:** 11
coloring paper **3:** 54
color mixing **6:** 4-6
composite materials **7:** 56, 57
composite wood **3:** 24
compounds of metals **2:** 4, 6; **9:** 36, 38, 43, 47, 48
compressed air **9:** 14, 28-31, 34, 35, 54
compressibility of water **8:** 31
compression molding **1:** 18
compression resistance in ceramics **4:** 8
concrete **4:** 10, 35, 39-41
condensation **8:** 16, 18-19, 49, 50; **9:** 16, 53
condensation polymer, condensation polymerization **1:** 43; **7:** 10, 14
conductivity. *See* electrical conductivity and heat (thermal) conductivity
conifers, coniferous trees **3:** 16, 48
contact adhesives **6:** 41, 52-53
contact lenses **1:** 40
continuous casting **2:** 17
continuous production tunnel kilns **4:** 30
convection **9:** 18, 22, 25, 27. *See also* heat convection
cooling towers **8:** 34
copolymer **1:** 38
copper **2:** 4, 5, 6, 9, 10, 14, 16, 17, 23, 24, 25, 26, 27, 28, 30, 36, 37, 38, 39, 40, 41, 43, 45, 53, 56; **4:** 47; **5:** 11
copper ore **2:** 5
copper oxide **5:** 11
cores **5:** 30, 31
corn glue **6:** 49
Corning Corporation **5:** 13
corrosion **2:** 28, 32; **8:** 27, 53, 54, 57
corrosion in glass **5:** 13, 14, 16, 17, 18
corrosion in water **8:** 53-54
corrosion resistance **1:** 29, 30, 43; **2:** 23, 24, 25, 26, 27, 28-34, 38, 49, 51; **4:** 32, 46, 54, 55, 57
corrugated iron **2:** 31
cotton **1:** 13, 51; **3:** 49, 55; **7:** 4, 7, 17, 19, 20, 21, 25, 43
covalent bonding **4:** 5; **8:** 8, 9
crankshaft **8:** 22
crease-resistant fabrics **7:** 17, 27, 42, 46. *See also* durable-, permanent-, and stay-pressed fabrics
creosote **3:** 24, 40; **6:** 36
creping **3:** 56
crimped materials **7:** 27, 37; **8:** 26
cristallo **5:** 37
critical angle **5:** 20
crockery **4:** 19, 24
cross linking **7:** 17
crown glass **5:** 39, 49
crucible glass **5:** 29-30
crucibles **2:** 47; **4:** 32
crude oil **1:** 6, 28; **6:** 7, 8, 10, 16, 26, 36; **9:** 45
crysocolla **2:** 5
crystal glass **5:** 37
Crystal Palace **2:** 56; **5:** 42
crystals and crystalline materials **2:** 3, 6, 13, 14, 18, 22; **4:** 6-8, 9, 19, 34, 35, 39, 43, 48, 50, 52; **5:** 4, 6, 14
cullet **5:** 42
curing concrete **4:** 39

curing rubber **1**: 9
cut glass **5**: 9
cutlery **2**: 31
cyanoacrylate **1**: 40; **6**: 50, 54
cylinder glass **5**: 40
cylinders **8**: 21, 22

D

Dacron® **1**: 50; **7**: 42
daggers **2**: 41
Dalton, John **9**: 11
Dalton's law **9**: 10
Damascus steel **2**: 41
damp-proof layer **8**: 28
Darby, Abraham 47
debarking machine **3**: 34
decay in wood **3**: 24, 30, 41, 43
deciduous trees **3**: 30
decolorizing glass **5**: 11, 36
decompose **7**: 7, 10, 14, 24, 33, 44
decomposition of plastics **1**: 24, 49
decomposition of water **8**: 17, 56
decompression sickness **9**: 42
decorative laminates **1**: 22
defibering **3**: 53
density of gases **9**: 9, 15
density of plastics **1**: 4, 24, 29, 32, 33
density of water **8**: 8, 12, 13, 20, 28, 31, 37, 39
density of wood **3**: 20-24, 27
dental cement **4**: 55-56
dental fillings **4**: 3, 55
desalination **8**: 41, 50-51
desalting **8**: 41. *See also* desalination
detergents **8**: 29, 30-31, 46, 55
deuterium **8**: 14
diamond **4**: 4, 6, 57
die casting **2**: 17
die extrusion **1**: 17, 18; **2**: 19
diene plastics **1**: 42, 43
dies **2**: 17, 19, 21, 39; **4**: 17, 28, 57
diffusion **8**: 39, 40; **9**: 17
dipping **1**: 21
direct dyeing **7**: 30
dishwasher-proof plastic containers **1**: 32
disperse dyeing **6**: 21-22
disposable plastics **1**: 14, 20, 23, 24, 33, 47, 51
dissociation in water **8**: 16, 47, 55(gloss)
dissolving substances in water **8**: 6, 42-57
distillation of air **9**: 36
distillation of water **8**: 49-51
distilled water **8**: 49, 50
doped ceramics **4**: 8, 45, 51, 52, 53
doping **4**: 6, 45
double glazing **5**: 26; **9**: 23
Douglas fir **3**: 16, 20
drafts **9**: 27
drawing **2**: 13, 19
drawing dies **2**: 19; **4**: 57
drawing fibers. *See* stretching fibers
drinking water supplies **8**: 6
drip-dry fabrics **1**: 47
dry cleaned **7**: 41
dry felting **3**: 45
dry ice **9**: 50
drying wood **3**: 23, 36, 37
dry-press process **4**: 28
dry spinning **7**: 34
ductile material **2**: 18
Dumas, Jean-Baptiste-André **5**: 38

durable-press fabrics **7**: 16-17. *See also* permanent- and stay-pressed fabrics
dyeing artificial fibers **7**: 37
dyeing metals **2**: 32
dyeing natural fibers **6**: 7, 17, 18, 20, 21, 24; **7**: 30
dyeing plastics **1**: 16, 39
dyeing synthetic fibers **6**: 17, 20, 21
dyes **6**: 4-26; **7**: 7, 30, 38
dyes and dyeing fibers **6**: 6, 7, 17, 21, 22, 23, 24; **7**: 7, 24, 25, 27, 29, 30, 37, 38, 41, 42, 45, 46, 47, 51, 52
dyes and papermaking **3**: 51, 54

E

early wood **3**: 14
earthenware **4**: 22, 23, 24, 25
eggshell paint **6**: 34
Egypt **5**: 28, 33
Egyptians **5**: 30
Eiffel Tower **2**: 54
eighteen-carat gold **2**: 26
elastic limit **2**: 20, 35
elasticity in materials **1**: 8, 56, 57; **2**: 20, 22, 35; **5**: 23; **7**: 4, 7, 37, 47, 57; **9**: 14, 28
elastic properties of wood **3**: 8, 19, 29
electrical conductivity **1**: 4, 13, 14; **2**: 4, 6, 9, 11, 25, 53; **4**: 6, 7, 8, 45, 46, 52-53, 56; **5**: 15, 18 ; **7**: 56, 57; **8**: 10, 44, 46-48; **9**: 21, 22
electrical insulation **1**: 13, 14, 29, 32, 35, 37, 44, 45; **3**: 28; **4**: 7, 22, 44, 46, 52, 56; **5**: 18; **8**: 46, 47; **9**: 21-22
electrical properties of glass **5**: 18
electrical transformers **2**: 10
electric arc furnace **2**: 49
electric arc welding **2**: 52
electrofloat process **5**: 50
electrolysis **8**: 47, 56
electrolytes **8**: 46, 48
electromagnet **2**: 9
electronics **4**: 44-45, 46, 52, 53
electrons **1**: 13; **2**: 6, 7, 9, 28, 30; **4**: 5, 7, 47, 52; **8**: 9, 47, 56
elements **2**: 4, 8; **8**: 4; **9**: 4. *See also* heating elements
Empire State Building **2**: 57
emulsion paints **6**: 33, 34
enamel paints **2**: 33; **6**: 38
enamels, enameling **2**: 24, 33, 49, 57; **4**: 23; **5**: 14; **6**: 38
energy **8**: 14, 16, 17, 23, 35
energy efficient glasses **5**: 15
engineered wood products **3**: 42
epoxy, epoxy resin **1**: 53, 54, 55
epoxy resin adhesives **6**: 50-51
epoxy resin varnishes **6**: 37
etching glass **5**: 17
ethylene **1**: 10, 17, 20, 28, 33, 35, 37, 41
ethylene-propylene **1**: 32
eucalyptus **3**: 15
evaporation **8**: 4, 6, 16, 18-19, 20, 42
exosphere **9**: 20
exothermic reaction **8**: 52
expansion properties of glass **5**: 19
external combustion engine **8**: 22
extrusion **1**: 17, 19; **2**: 13, 19; **7**: 4, 10, 14, 32, 33, 34, 36, 37, 38, 42, 45, 46
eyeglasses **1**: 20; **5**: 26, 55

F

fabrics **1**: 13, 31, 44, 45, 47; **7**: 8, 10, 12, 15, 19, 20, 22, 25, 33
fat **8**: 30, 45, 46, 52
feldspars **4**: 15, 17, 22, 26, 29
felt **3**: 51
felting **3**: 45, 46; **7**: 28
ferric oxide **5**: 11
ferrites **4**: 48, 49
ferromagnetic metals **2**: 10
ferrous oxide **5**: 11
fertilizers **8**: 6; **9**: 36, 38, 41
fiberboard **3**: 45
fiberglass **1**: 16, 23; **2**: 12; **5**: 54, 57; **7**: 6, 54; **9**: 23. *See also* glass fiber
fibers **1**: 7, 18, 23, 25, 31, 39, 44, 46, 47, 48, 50, 51, 56; **3**: 4, 18, 22, 23, 24, 26, 28, 45, 46; **6**: 6, 17, 22, 23, 24; **7**: 4 AND THROUGHOUT; **9**: 23, 52
fibers in papermaking **3**: 4, 46-57
fibrin **7**: 28
filaments **6**: 41; **7**: 4, 28, 32, 33, 34, 47
filler **3**: 54; **4**: 15, 29, 30, 33, 39, 55; **6**: 9
finishes on paper **3**: 53-54
fir **3**: 16, 20
fire extinguishers **8**: 36, 37; **9**: 50
fire resistance **1**: 12, 14, 38, 46, 48, 52; **7**: 8, 14, 34, 45, 54
firing bricks **4**: 28-29, 30-31
firing ceramics **4**: 18-19, 20, 28, 29, 30, 31, 46
firing temperature **4**: 20, 30
fishing line **1**: 48, 49; **7**: 49, 54
flak jacket **2**: 42
flame-resistance in wood **3**: 27
flash distillation **8**: 50-51
flat glass **5**: 33, 34, 39, 40, 42, 49-52, 53
flat paint **6**: 34
flax **3**: 49; **7**: 19, 20, 21
fleece **7**: 26
flexibility in fibers **7**: 6, 7
flint **4**: 5
float glass **5**: 49, 50, 51
float glass process **5**: 50-51
floating **8**: 8, 38-39, 51
fluorescent lamps and tubes **4**: 51, 52; **9**: 55, 56
fluorine **1**: 10, 41
fluorite **4**: 50
fluxes **2**: 40; **4**: 15, 16, 27, 29; **5**: 8, 9, 16
foamed polystyrene **1**: 14, 23, 32, 34
foaming agents **1**: 21; **8**: 37
foams and foamed plastics **1**: 14, 21-22, 23, 32, 33, 34, 56, 57
food coloring **6**: 24, 25-26
forests **3**: 10, 17, 30, 31, 32, 56
forging **2**: 13, 20, 23 41
former **5**: 8
Formica® **1**: 44
forming bricks **4**: 17, 28, 29
fossil fuels **9**: 38, 47, 48, 49
fractional distillation **9**: 36
fracturing in ceramics **4**: 5, 8, 9
fracturing in glass **5**: 6, 12, 13, 24
frame for construction **3**: 5, 7, 38, 44
freeze-dried ceramics **4**: 43
freeze-dry food **9**: 41
freezing **8**: 16, 17
freezing point of water **8**: 8, 31, 49, 50
fresh water **8**: 6
frit **5**: 52; **6**: 39

froth flotation **8**: 51
froth separation **8**: 51
fuel, wood **3**: 5, 6, 28
fumes **1**: 14, 25
furnaces **2**: 12, 41. *See also* glass furnaces
furniture **1**: 14, 22; **3**: 5, 17, 19, 22, 32, 36, 42, 43
fuses **2**: 26
fusing ceramics **4**: 9, 19, 20, 24, 30

G

galvanic protection **2**: 30-32
galvanized iron **2**: 57
galvanized steel **1**: 13;l **2**: 30, 31
galvanizing **2**: 6, 31
gang saw **3**: 34
gaseous state of water. *See* water vapor
gases **8**: 4, 5, 6, 7, 16, 17, 24, 42, 47, 56, 57; **9**: 4 AND THROUGHOUT
gas laws **9**: 8-10
gas-proof plastics **1**: 37, 51
gears **2**: 21
gelatin **6**: 48
gel spinning **7**: 34, 36
giant molecules **7**: 4
gilding metals **2**: 24
ginning **7**: 25
glass **1**: 12, 13, 23, 38, 40, 44, 52; **2**: 4, 33, 50, 56; **4**: 4, 9, 19, 20, 21, 22, 25, 26, 30, 32, 40; **5**: 4 AND THROUGHOUT; **6**: 38
glass adhesives **6**: 55
glass beads **6**: 39
glass blowing **5**: 33
glass ceramics **4**: 53; **5**: 14, 19
glass enamel **2**: 33; **6**: 38
glass fiber **1**: 16, 22, 23, 53; **4**: 57; **7**: 6, 53-54, 55, 56; **5**: 13, 54
glass furnaces **5**: 14, 29, 32, 36, 41, 42, 43, 50, 55
glassmaker's soap **5**: 36
glass microfiber **7**: 6
glass powder **6**: 38, 39
glass transition temperature **7**: 44
glassy state **5**: 5
glazes and glazing **4**: 9, 20-21, 22, 23, 24, 25, 29, 31, 51; **5**: 13, 14, 24; **6**: 38
global warming **9**: 49
gloss paint **6**: 29, 31, 33, 34, 35
glucose **3**: 10; **7**: 12
glue **6**: 10, 41, 48-49
glulam **3**: 42
gobs **5**: 32, 43
gold **2**: 4, 5, 9, 10, 11, 25, 26, 28, 36, 37, 39, 40; **8**: 55
Golden Gate Bridge **2**: 56-57
gold nuggets **2**: 36, 37
Goop **6**: 56
grain, in wood **3**: 9, 16, 17, 18, 24
graphite **4**: 4, 6, 7, 57
gravity **8**: 25, 32; **9**: 14
greaseproof paper **3**: 56
Greece **5**: 28
Greeks **2**: 42, 43; **4**: 13, 35; **8**: 4
greenhouse effect **9**: 21, 49, 50
ground glass **5**: 17, 36, 49, 56
groundwater **8**: 7, 55
growth rings **3**: 13, 14, 16, 20
gum arabic **6**: 49
gums **3**: 10, 12, 13, 14, 20, 22, 27, 46, 54; **6**: 49; **7**: 19, 20

gunmetal **2**: 25
gypsum **4**: 34, 37, 38

H

hairs **7**: 6, 7, 9, 10, 21, 22, 25, 26, 27
Hall, Charles M. **2**: 50
hammering metals **2**: 20, 37, 39, 40, 41, 43
hard water **8**: 55
hardness in metals **2**: 8
hardwoods **3**: 16, 17, 18, 19, 22, 23, 28, 48
harvesting trees **3**: 30-32
HDPE. *See* high-density polyethylene
headsaw **3**: 34, 36
heartwood **3**: 12, 13, 14
heat—effect on plastics **1**: 4, 11, 12, 13, 14, 21, 24, 25, 35, 37, 43, 44, 48, 52
heating elements **4**: 52, 53; **8**: 38, 55
heating metals **2**: 12, 13, 20, 21, 22-23, 26, 40, 41
heat (thermal) conductivity **1**: 14; **2**: 4, 6, 9, 33; **4**: 4; **5**: 7, 12, 19; **8**: 32-35, 37; **9**: 15, 22, 26, 27
heat (thermal) insulation **1**: 14, 21, 23, 34, 43, 53, 57; **3**: 8, 27-28, 57; **4**: 42; **5**: 7, 18; **7**: 27, 36, 46, 54; **9**: 22-23
heat capacity **8**: 32. *See also* thermal capacity
heat convection **8**: 37-38; **9**: 25, 27
heat storage **8**: 32-35
heavy water **8**: 14, 15
helium **9**: 18, 54-55
hematite **2**: 5
hemp **7**: 11, 19, 20, 21
Héroult, Paul-Louis-Toussaint **2**: 50
high-density polyethylene (HDPE) **1**: 26, 29, 30, 31, 32
high-k glass **5**: 18
Hindenburg **9**: 51
holograms **5**: 22
hot glue **1**: 42
hot rolling **2**: 18
hotworking **2**: 13, 14
household water systems **8**: 33
hovercrafts **9**: 32-34
human hair **7**: 6
humidity **9**: 21, 26, 52, 53
hydration **4**: 35; **8**: 56
hydraulics and hydraulic action **8**: 31
hydroelectric power generation **8**: 35
hydrofluoric acid etching **5**: 17
hydrogen **8**: 8, 9, 14, 16, 47, 52, 54, 55-56; **9**: 10, 18, 19, 41, 49, 51, 54
hydrogen bonds and bonding **6**: 20; **7**: 17, 39, 51; **8**: 11-13, 14, 36
hydrogen chloride **1**: 35
hydrolysis **7**: 46
hydrophilic substances **8**: 30, 45
hydrophobic substances **8**: 29, 30, 45
hygrometer **9**: 52
hypocaust **9**: 24, 25

I

ice **8**: 8, 11, 12, 13, 16, 17, 24, 25
Illing, Moritz **3**: 53
immiscibility **8**: 28
impermeable ceramics **4**: 20, 22. *See also* watertight ceramics
impurities in water **8**: 7, 48, 49
indigo **6**: 11, 13, 14, 15, 20, 21
indium oxide **4**: 53

Industrial Revolution **2**: 43, 46-49, 54; **4**: 13; **7**: 22; **8**: 21
inert gases **9**: 21, 41, 42, 53, 55
ingrain dyeing **6**: 21, 22; **7**: 38
injection molding **1**: 18, 25, 32, 50
inks **6**: 8, 9
inner bark **3**: 12, 13
inorganic materials **6**: 9
insulation. *See* electrical insulation and heat (thermal) insulation
integrated circuits **4**: 8, 45
International Space Station **5**: 52
ionic bonding **4**: 5
ionic substances **8**: 42, 46
ions **2**: 6, 7; **4**: 6, 7, 8, 15; **8**: 9, 40, 41, 42, 43, 44, 46, 47
iron **2**: 4, 5, 9, 10, 11, 12, 16, 18, 21, 22, 23, 25, 30, 31, 37, 38, 39, 40, 41, 43, 44, 45, 46, 47, 49, 54, 55, 560, 41, 43, 46, 47; **4**: 16, 24, 27, 36, 38, 48; **8**: 53, 54
Iron Age **2**: 38-41
ironed **7**: 33
ironing fibers **7**: 16-17, 33, 41, 44, 49
ironwood **3**: 20
iron ore **2**: 5
iron oxide **2**: 5, 40; **4**: 38, 49; **5**: 8
iron staining **4**: 16, 24, 27
irrigation **8**: 6
isocyanates **6**: 43
isoprene **1**: 6, 8
isotopes **8**: 14
ivory **1**: 46

J

Jesse Littleton **5**: 13
jewelry **2**: 24, 25, 26, 36, 37, 39, 50
jiggering **4**: 25
jute **7**: 19, 20

K

kaolin, kaolinite **3**: 54; **4**: 14, 16, 24, 25
kapok **7**: 20
keratin **7**: 26
Kevlar® **1**: 48; **2**: 42; **7**: 8, 34, 50, 51
kiln drying of wood **3**: 36, 37
kilns **4**: 9, 19, 27, 32, 35, 37, 38, 51; **5**: 14, 38
kinetic energy **8**: 35
knapping **5**: 7
knitting **7**: 22, 23
knots **3**: 18, 20, 26
kraft process **3**: 51, 52
krypton **9**: 18, 54, 56

L

lacquers **1**: 11, 53; **2**: 29; **6**: 40, 42
laminated glass **5**: 21, 26, 27, 28
laminated windshields and safety glass **1**: 23, 37, 37
laminates **1**: 22, 23, 44; **3**: 24 **6**: 50
lanolin **7**: 26
lasers **4**: 52; **5**: 57
latent heat **8**: 17
latent heat **9**: 16, 52
late wood **3**: 14
latex **1**: 8; **3**: 54; **6**: 29, 49
latex paints **6**: 29, 34-35
lathed glass **5**: 30
lattice **8**: 12, 17
laundry powder **6**: 3, 24

LCDs. *See* liquid crystal displays
LDPE. *See* low-density polyethylene
lead **2:** 10, 11, 24, 25, 40, 42, 43, 44
lead crystal glass **5:** 37
lead monoxide **5:** 11
lead oxide **4:** 53; **5:** 8, 11
lead-silicate glass **5:** 22, 55
leaf fiber **7:** 19
leather **6:** 17
lenses **4:** 50; **5:** 9, 21, 22, 26, 55, 56
Liberty Bell **2:** 14
lift, using air **9:** 32, 34, 35
light bulb filaments **2:** 9, 21, 53
light bulbs **5:** 13, 43, 44-45
lightfast pigments **6:** 9
lignin **3:** 10, 46, 48, 50, 51
lime **4:** 13, 35, 38; **5:** 8, 9, 10, 13, 16, 17, 18, 22, 29, 30, 38
limestone **4:** 35, 36, 37, 38; **5:** 9, 38
linen, linen fibers **3:** 49; **7:** 20, 21
linseed oil **1:** 53; **6:** 28, 37
liquefying gases **9:** 14, 36, 41
liquid crystal displays (LCDs) **4:** 53
liquid oxygen **9:** 36
liquid state of water **8:** 8, 15, 16, 19, 20, 21
liquids **5:** 5; **9:** 5, 12; **8:** 4, 5, 14, 16, 17, 19
lithium **2:** 27, 53
lithium oxide **5:** 9
lodestone **4:** 48
logs **3:** 5, 8, 23, 30, 31, 32, 34, 35, 36, 42
logwood **6:** 12
low-density polyethylene (LDPE) **1:** 26, 27, 28, 29, 30
lubricant **4:** 6, 7, 57
lumber **3:** 34
Lycra® **7:** 52

M

machinability of metal alloys **2:** 23
machine-made glass **5:** 42-57
madder plant **6:** 12, 13
magnesia **5:** 8, 9
magnesium **2:** 5, 10, 25, 26, 27, 32, 50
magnetic ceramics **4:** 48-49
magnetic properties of glass **5:** 15
magnetism in ceramics **4:** 48-49
magnetism in metals **2:** 9-10
magnetite **2:** 9; **4:** 48
magnets **4:** 44, 48
mandrel **5:** 53
manganese **5:** 11, 21
man-made fibers **7:** 12, 31
maple **3:** 27
marine ply **3:** 43
Martin, Pierre and Émile **2:** 47
massicot **6:** 12
matting of fibers **7:** 21, 28
mechanical properties of glass **5:** 22-24
medicines **8:** 48
melamine **1:** 22, 45, 53; **6:** 29, 40
melamine-formaldehyde **1:** 22
melting **8:** 8, 11, 12, 14, 16, 17, 49
melting point of water **8:** 11, 49
melting points of metals **2:** 6
melt spinning **7:** 34, 36
mercuric oxide decomposition **9:** 12
mercury **2:** 10, 43
mesosphere **9:** 20
metal fatigue **2:** 27, 35
metallic glasses **5:** 15

metalloids **2:** 8
metal ores **2:** 5, 9, 37, 38
metal oxides **4:** 20, 27, 48; **5:** 11
metallurgy **2:** 12
metals **1:** 4, 5, 12, 13, 15, 16, 23, 48, 52, 55, 56, 57; **2:** 4 AND THROUGHOUT; **3:** 6, 8, 26; **4:** 4, 7, 8, 9, 16, 30, 46, 48, 51, 56; **5:** 6, 15; **8:** 53-55
methane **9:** 18
methyl orange **6:** 14
microelectronic circuits **4:** 53
microfiber **5:** 57; **7:** 6, 18, 19, 46
Middle Ages **2:** 39, 43, 44
mild steel **2:** 29, 49
milk glue **6:** 49
millefiori **5:** 33
minerals **4:** 4, 34, 50; **5:** 4. *See also* clay minerals
mineral water **8:** 7
mining **2:** 5
minting **2:** 39
mirrors **5:** 22, 56
mixtures and water **8:** 19, 32, 42, 49
mixtures in metals **2:** 6, 23
mixtures, mixture of gases **9:** 4, 10, 16-17
modacrylic **7:** 36
moderator **8:** 14
moisture in the atmosphere **9:** 52-53
mold, molding **1:** 9, 12, 18, 19, 20, 21
molded glass **5:** 30
molds and molding **2:** 14, 15, 16, 17, 39, 41; **4:** 9, 12, 17, 28, 29, 43; **5:** 30, 43, 44, 46, 48, 54, 55
molecules **8:** 8, 24. *See also* water molecules
molecules and molecular structures **1:** 6, 7, 10, 11, 33; **7:** 4, 8, 9, 10, 12, 13, 14, 17, 30, 32, 34, 37, 44; **9:** 7, 8, 9, 12-14, 15, 16, 17, 18, 37, 44, 53
monomers **1:** 10
mordant **3:** 53; **6:** 7, 10, 12, 20; **7:** 30
mortar **4:** 16, 35, 38, 39
mosaics **4:** 13, 14, 21; **5:** 33
mud **4:** 11
muskets **2:** 45

N

nail manufacture **2:** 56
nail polish **1:** 46
native copper **2:** 37
native gold **2:** 4, 36
native metals **2:** 4, 36
natural adhesives **3:** 46, 51, 53, 54; **6:** 48-49
natural dyes **6:** 7, 11-13
natural fibers **1:** 13; **6:** 7, 17, 18, 20, 21, 24; **7:** 7, 9, 10, 12, 14, 19-30, 31, 32, 34, 36, 38, 44, 46
natural gas **1:** 17, 28; **9:** 48
natural polymers **1:** 6, 7, 8-9; **7:** 10-12, 14
natural resins **3:** 10, 13, 14, 20, 23, 27, 46, 52, 54, 56; **6:** 37
natural rubber **1:** 7, 8-9, 12, 13, 42
natural varnishes **6:** 37
neon **9:** 18, 54, 57
neoprene **1:** 42; **6:** 52
nets **7:** 22, 44, 49
neutrons **2:** 6
newspaper, newsprint papers **3:** 46, 52, 56
nickel **2:** 9, 24, 26, 30; **4:** 47, 48; **5:** 11
nitric oxide **9:** 30

nitrogen cycle **9:** 38
nitrogen dioxide **9:** 13, 19, 21, 39, 40
nitrogen, nitrogen gas **1:** 21; **9:** 18, 36, 37-42
nitrogen oxides (Nox) **9:** 13, 18, 19, 21, 30, 37, 38, 39, 40, 46
nitrous oxide **9:** 18
noble gases **9:** 53-57
nonflammable gases **9:** 54
noniron plastics **1:** 45, 47
nonmetals **2:** 6, 8; **5:** 18
nonstick plastics **1:** 10, 41
Nox. *See* nitrogen oxides
nucleating agent **5:** 14
nylon **1:** 13, 48-49, 50; **6:** 8, 20; **7:** 10, 14, 30, 31, 32–33, 34, 35, 36, 37, 47-51, 52, 57

O

oak **3:** 5, 17, 18, 19, 28
obsidian **5:** 7
oceans, ocean water **8:** 4, 6, 37
oil **8:** 28, 32
oil paint, oil-based paints **6:** 29, 35
oils **3:** 10; **9:** 45, 48, 49, 54. *See also* crude oil
olefin, olefin fibers **7:** 36, 52
opacity in materials **1:** 24, 30, 33; **3:** 51, 54; **5:** 7, 14
open-pit mining **2:** 5
optic fiber casings **1:** 12
optic fibers, optical fibers, optical glass fibers **5:** 56-57; **7:** 55
optical properties of glass **5:** 20
optical switches **4:** 44
optics **4:** 44-45, 50
ores **2:** 5, 9, 37, 38
oriented strand board **3:** 42, 44
Orlon® **1:** 39; **7:** 45
osmosis **8:** 40-41
Otis, Elisha **2:** 57
outer bark **3:** 12
oven glass **5:** 9
ovenware **5:** 12
oxide film, oxide coat **2:** 10, 11, 29, 30, 32
oxodizing agent **8:** 7, 53
oxygen **1:** 13, 35, 37, 43, 53, 54, 55, 57; **2:** 4, 6, 10, 38, 52; **4:** 6, 7, 8, 14, 27, 53; **8:** 4, 7, 8, 9, 10, 14, 37, 42, 46, 53, 55-56; **9:** 10, 11, 12, 18, 19, 20, 21, 36, 38, 39, 41, 43-45, 47, 48, 51, 54, 55
oxygen cycle **9:** 43
ozone **1:** 29, 57; **9:** 19, 20, 21, 44

P

packaging material **1:** 21, 22, 29, 30, 32, 33, 34, 37, 57; **3:** 46, 51, 57
pad-dry dyeing **6:** 22, 23
painting metals **2:** 28, 29, 33
painting wood **3:** 8, 41
paints **1:** 37, 41, 45, 53p; **6:** 4-16, 27-40
palladium **2:** 26; **4:** 46
PAN. *See* polyacrylonitrile
panning **2:** 4
paper **1:** 22, 23, 37, 44, 46; **3:** 4, 11, 34, 46-57; **6:** 9; **7:** 8, 19, 20, 41; **8:** 26, 29
papermaking **3:** 50-54
paper stock **3:** 54
paper towels **3:** 56
paper weight **3:** 46

papier-mâché **6**: 42
papyrus **3**: 46, 47; **6**: 42
Parkesine **1**: 46
particleboard **1**: 44; **3**: 44
paste, flour-based **6**: 42
patina **2**: 28
PC. *See* polycarbonate
PE. *See* polyethylene
periodic table **2**: 8, 50
permanent hardness **8**: 55
permanent magnets **2**: 10
permanent-press fabrics **7**: 16-17, 44. *See also* durable- and stay-pressed fabrics
Perspex® **1**: 38, 39
PET or PETE. *See* polyethylene terephthalate
petrochemicals **1**: 12; **7**: 8
petroleum, petroleum products **1**: 12; **7**: 12, 31, 52
phenolic varnishes **6**: 37
phenols, phenolic resin **1**: 21, 43, 44
phlogiston **9**: 51
Phoenicians **5**: 32
phosphoric acid **5**: 17
phosphors **4**: 51, 52
photochemical smog **9**: 40
photochromic glasses **5**: 22
photosynthesis **9**: 21, 43, 48
piezoelectrics **4**: 47-48
pigments **1**: 16, 24, 30, 37, 53; **3**: 54; **4**: 51; **6**: 6-10, 11, 27, 29, 40; **7**: 38
Pilkington, Alastair **5**: 49
pine **3**: 16, 23, 27
pistols **2**: 45
pistons **8**: 21, 22
pith **3**: 13
planks **3**: 34, 36, 37, 39
plaster **4**: 18, 34
plaster of Paris **4**: 34
plastering **4**: 34
plastic bags **1**: 4, 10, 13, 18, 22, 28, 29
plastic bottles **1**: 4, 15, 19, 20, 24, 25, 26, 29, 30, 31, 32, 50, 51
plastic change **2**: 22, 35
plastic film **1**: 7, 18, 29, 37, 46,47
plasticity **1**: 4
plasticity in ceramics **4**: 8, 28, 29
plasticity in glass **5**: 23
plasticity in wood **3**: 19
plasticizers **1**: 15, 16, 21; **7**: 17
plastic metal **6**: 51
plastics **1**: 4 AND THROUGHOUT; **2**: 4, 12, 14, 33; **3**: 6; **4**: 43, 49, 56; **5**: 26; **6**: 41, 43, 49; **7**: 8, 32; **9**: 41, 50
plastic sheet **1**: 6, 7, 11, 18, 20, 22, 23, 37, 38, 42, 44, 47, 50
plastic wood **6**: 51
plate glass **5**: 41, 49
plating **2**: 30, 32
platinum **2**: 10, 11, 21; **4**: 43, 57; **8**: 55
pleats **7**: 16, 17, 44
Plexiglas® **1**: 38
pliable properties of wood **3**: 19, 22
plows, plowshares **2**: 44, 46
plumbing **2**: 43
plutonium oxides **4**: 54
plywood **1**: 22, 44; **3**: 24, 42, 43
PMMA. *See* polymethyl methacrylate
pneumatic devices **9**: 29-31
pneumatic trough **9**: 10
polar solvent **8**: 43

polarity in water **8**: 9, 10, 11
poles **3**: 33
polish **3**: 8
polishing **5**: 24, 30, 49, 50, 51
pollution **8**: 51, 57. *See also* air pollution
pollution control **2**: 11
polyacrylonitrile (PAN) **7**: 45
polyamides **1**: 48; **7**: 47, 49
polycarbonate (PC) **1**: 13, 52, 53
polychloroethylene **1**: 10
polyester **6**: 21
polyester fiber **1**: 13, 47; **7**: 10, 14, 17, 18, 31, 33, 34, 36, 42-44, 46, 49, 50, 51, 54
polyethers **1**: 13, 22, 50-54
polyethylene (PE) **1**: 4, 10, 11, 20, 21, 22, 26, 27, 28-30, 31, 32; **7**: 33, 52; **8**: 28
polyethylene terephthalate (PETE or PET) **1**: 20, 24, 25, 26, 50-51; **6**: 21; **7**: 32, 37, 42
polyisoprene **1**: 8
polymer industry **1**: 8
polymerization **1**: 10; **7**: 10, 14, 15, 49
polymer membrane **8**: 41
polymers **1**: 6, 7, 10, 13, 14, 15, 16, 27, 28, 37, 38, 41; **3**: 10; **6**: 17, 28, 43, 49; **7**: 9, 10-14, 31, 32, 33
polymethyl methacrylate (PMMA) **1**: 40-41
polypropylene (PP) **1**: 11, 20, 26, 27, 31-33; **7**: 52
polypropylene fibers **7**: 33, 38, 52
polystyrene (PS) **1**: 10, 14, 20, 21, 23, 24, 26, 33-34, 47, 54; **6**: 57
polytetrafluoroethylene (PTFE) **1**: 10, 41
polyurethane adhesives **6**: 50
polyurethane fibers **7**: 52
polyurethanes **1**: 21, 56-57
polyurethane varnishes **6**: 37
polyvinyl acetate (PVA, PVAc) **1**: 37; **6**: 54
polyvinyl acetate (PVA) adhesive **6**: 54-55, 57
polyvinyl acetate (PVA) glue **1**: 37
polyvinyl chloride (PVC) **1**: 10, 13, 14, 15, 16, 20, 21, 25, 26, 35, 36, 37. *See also* vinyl
polyvinylidene (PVDC) **1**: 36, 37
poplar **3**: 17
porcelain **2**: 26, 57; **4**: 22, 25-26, 52, 56
porcelain enamel **4**: 23; **5**: 14
pores **7**: 30
porous ceramics **4**: 18, 30, 31, 40, 55
Portland cement **4**: 35, 37, 38
Portland cement plant **4**: 36-37
Post-it® Notes **6**: 54
posts **3**: 33
potash **5**: 8, 9
potassium **2**: 5, 8, 10
potato glue **6**: 49
potential energy **8**: 35
pottery **4**: 4, 17, 31
powder coatings **6**: 40
powder forming **2**: 13, 21
powder glass **5**: 52
powder paints **6**: 12, 13
powders **4**: 9, 34, 35, 37, 38, 43-44, 46, 48, 49, 50, 51, 52, 55
PP. *See* polypropylene
precipitation **8**: 55, 57
preservatives **3**: 30, 33, 40, 41; **6**: 36
preserving wood **3**: 30, 40-41

pressing **2**: 20
pressure **9**: 5, 8, 12, 13
pressure cooker **8**: 21
pressure of a gas **9**: 8, 9, 14, 15. *See also* air pressure
pressure-sensitive adhesives (PSAs) **6**: 54
pressure-treated wood **3**: 33, 40
primary colors **6**: 4
primers **6**: 28, 30, 33
Prince Rupert's Drop **5**: 10
properties of gases **9**: 12-17
properties of wood **3**: 19-29
propylene **1**: 11, 28
protective clothing **1**: 14, 48
protective coatings **6**: 27-40
proteins **6**: 17, 48, 49; **7**: 4, 10, 26, 28
protons **2**: 6
PS. *See* polystyrene
PSAs. *See* pressure-sensitive adhesives
PTFE. *See* polytetrafluoroethylene
pugging **4**: 28
pulp fibers **3**: 53
pulp, pulp production **3**: 32, 45, 46, 48, 51-54, 56
pumping engine **8**: 21
pumps **9**: 5, 6, 8, 28
pure liquids **8**: 49
pure water **8**: 6, 49
PVA adhesive **6**: 54-55, 57
PVA glue **1**: 37
PVA, PVAc. *See* polyvinyl acetate
PVC. *See* polyvinyl chloride
PVDC. *See* polyvinylidene
Pyrex® **5**: 12, 13

Q

quartzite **5**: 9
quenching **2**: 41

R

radiation **9**: 21, 22, 27
radiators **9**: 26, 27
radioactive water **8**: 14, 15
radiometer **9**: 14
radon **9**: 54, 56
raffia **7**: 19
rags, rag fibers **3**: 49
railroads, railroad stations and tracks **2**: 17, 18, 48, 49, 54
rain, rainwater **8**: 5, 57
rare earths **4**: 51
Ravenscroft, George **5**: 37
rayon **1**: 47, 48, 51; **3**: 50
rayon fiber **7**: 10, 12, 13, 17, 24, 31, 36, 37, 39-41, 57
rays **3**: 12, 14
reactive **9**: 43
reactive dyes **7**: 30
reactivity of metals **2**: 10-11
reactivity of water **8**: 6, 16, 53, 54
reactivity series **2**: 10; **8**: 54
ready-mixed concrete **4**: 39
recycling **1**: 12, 20, 23-26, 51; **3**: 56-57; **4**: 16; **5**: 3, 6, 41, 42
red oak **3**: 18
reducing agent **8**: 7
redwood **3**: 11, 13, 16
refiners **3**: 53
reflective paints **6**: 39
refraction in glass **5**: 20
refractive index of glass **5**: 21, 37, 55, 56

refractory bricks **4:** 31, 32, 33
refractory, refractory materials **4:** 6, 24, 31, 32-33
refrigerants **8:** 33; **9:** 41, 50
regenerated fibers **7:** 12, 31
reinforced concrete **4:** 40
reinforced fiber **4:** 10
reinforcers **1:** 15, 16; **7:** 57
reinforcing plastics **1:** 15, 16, 23, 44
repositionable adhesives **6:** 54
resin enamel **2:** 33; **6:** 38
Resin Identification Code **1:** 25, 26
resins **1:** 6, 11, 16, 22, 44, 53; **2:** 33; **4:** 43, 55, 56; **6:** 27, 37; **7:** 53, 54, 56, 57. *See also* natural resins and synthetic resins
respiration **9:** 12, 43, 48
respositionable adhesives **6:** 54
rifles **2:** 44, 45
rifling **2:** 45
rising damp **8:** 27
rivets **2:** 43, 52
road materials **4:** 41
Robert, Nicolas-Louis **3:** 46
rocks **8:** 4, 5, 6, 7
rocks and metals **2:** 4, 5, 36, 37, 38, 40, 43, 46, 50
rod glass **5:** 53
rolled glass **5:** 10
rolling **2:** 13, 17, 18, 23
rolling mill **2:** 18, 49
rolls of paper **3:** 51
Roman armor **2:** 40, 43
Romans **2:** 38, 40, 41, 42, 43, 55; **4:** 13, 35; **5:** 34, 36, 39, 49; **9:** 25
roof tiles **4:** 10, 16, 21
rope **7:** 19, 20, 22, 44, 48, 49
rosin **3:** 53
rotary saws **3:** 37
rough sawing **3:** 34-36
rubber **1:** 6, 7, 8, 9, 12, 13, 15, 21, 29, 42, 43, 56; **6:** 9, 49, 52; **7:** 37
rubber tree **1:** 8
ruby, synthetic **4:** 52
rugs **6:** 14; **7:** 27
rust **2:** 11, 27, 28, 29, 30; **8:** 53
rust-preventative surface coatings **6:** 28, 29, 30, 33
ruthenium dioxide **4:** 53

S
sacks, sacking **7:** 11, 20, 21
saffron **6:** 13
salt, salts **8:** 4, 5, 6, 7, 19, 40, 41, 42, 43, 44, 45, 46, 47, 48, 50, 55
sand **4:** 10, 12, 13, 15, 16, 17, 22, 29, 33, 36, 38, 39; **5:** 4, 8, 29
sap **3:** 14, 22, 47
sapphire **4:** 50
sapwood **3:** 10, 12, 13, 14
satin paint **6:** 34
saturated air **8:** 18
saturated solutions **8:** 44
sawdust **3:** 34
sawmill **3:** 23, 31, 34-35
sawn timber **3:** 8, 23, 36, 37
sculpting wood **3:** 8, 9
sealants **1:** 55; **6:** 43, 50, 56
seawater **8:** 7, 9, 19, 41, 42, 47, 50
selenium oxide **5:** 11
semiconductors **5:** 15
semigloss paint **6:** 34

semimetals **2:** 8
semipermeable membranes **8:** 40, 41
sensors **4:** 53
sewage **8:** 6, 41, 51
shakes **3:** 20, 26
shales **4:** 15, 28, 29, 30, 38
shaped glass **5:** 54
sheet glass **5:** 10
sheet-metal **2:** 13, 18, 20
shellac **1:** 6
shingles **3:** 8
shot **2:** 45
siding **3:** 7, 22
Siemens, Friedrich **2:** 47
silica **4:** 15, 38, 46, 57; **5:** 8
silica glasses **5:** 8, 9, 52
silicon **1:** 27, 43, 55; **4:** 14, 36, 37
silicon carbide **4:** 57
silicon chips **4:** 4, 6, 42, 45; **9:** 55
silicon dioxide **4:** 5, 38; **5:** 8
silicone-based adhesives and sealants **1:** 53, 55; **6:** 50, 54, 56-57
silk **1:** 6; **6:** 17; **7:** 4, 6, 10, 19, 21, 28-29; **8:** 29
silk cocoons **6:** 41; **7:** 28
silk substitute **7:** 46
silkworm **6:** 41; **7:** 4, 28
silver **2:** 4, 9, 10, 11, 25, 26, 36, 37, 39, 40, 43; **4:** 46; **8:** 55
silver halide **5:** 22
silver oxide **5:** 11
sinter, sintering **2:** 21; **4:** 9, 44
sisal, sisal fibers **3:** 47; **7:** 19
sizing **3:** 51, 53
skateboard wheels **1:** 56, 57
skein **7:** 22
skyscrapers **2:** 56, 57
slag **2:** 24, 40, 41
slip casting **4:** 17
smell **9:** 17
smelting **2:** 38
soap **8:** 30-31, 46, 55
soda **5:** 8, 9, 10, 17, 18, 22, 29, 38
soda-lime glass **5:** 8, 11, 12, 13, 19, 21, 23, 37, 38, 42, 48
sodium **2:** 5, 7, 10
sodium carbonate **5:** 8
sodium nitrate **5:** 11
sodium oxide **5:** 9
soft-mud process **4:** 28
softwoods, softwood forests **3:** 16, 17, 30, 48, 50
solar cells **5:** 52
solder **2:** 25
solidification **8:** 16
solids **5:** 5; **8:** 4, 5, 16, 17, 24; **9:** 5, 12
solubility of substances in water **8:** 45
solutes **8:** 41, 42
solution **8:** 6, 19, 32, 40, 42, 44
solvay process **5:** 38
solvents **1:** 39, 53; **6:** 27, 33, 34, 35, 37, 38, 40, 52, 54, 57; **8:** 6, 10, 41, 42, 43
sound and wood **3:** 8, 29-30
sound insulation **3:** 8, 29, 30
sound in water **8:** 39
sound-proofing **3:** 29
Space Shuttle **4:** 42; **5:** 52; **7:** 57
space suits **7:** 50-51
spandex **1:** 57; **7:** 36, 52
special fibers **7:** 53-57
speciality plastics **1:** 13

spectrum **5:** 20
spinneret **7:** 32, 34, 35, 36, 37, 41, 42, 45, 46, 47
spinning **1:** 7, 25; **7:** 7, 9, 21, 22, 34-36, 37, 40, 41
spinning bobbins **7:** 21
spinning wheels **7:** 21
springwood **3:** 14
spruce **3:** 16
stabilizers **1:** 15, 16; **5:** 8, 9, 13, 16
stained glass **5:** 34
stainless steel **2:** 19, 24, 27, 31, 32, 34
stains, paint **6:** 32, 34, 36
stalactite **8:** 57
stannite **2:** 37
staple **7:** 21, 25, 40
starch glues **3:** 43; **6:** 49
states of matter **5:** 5; **8:** 16
states of water **8:** 16
static electricity buildup **7:** 45, 52
Statue of Liberty **2:** 14, 28
stay-pressed fabrics **1:** 51. *See also* durable- and permanent-press fabrics
stealth technology **4:** 49
steam **8:** 16, 19, 20, 21
steam-driven engines **2:** 47, 49
steam engines **8:** 21-23
steam heating **3:** 22, 36, 43
steam turbines **8:** 23, 34
steel **1:** 7, 13, 15, 48; **2:** 10, 11, 13, 17, 18, 19, 22, 23, 24, 27, 28, 29, 30, 31, 32, 34, 39, 41, 42, 43, 45, 46, 47, 49, 50, 51, 54, 56, 57
sterling silver **2:** 25, 26
stiff-mud process **4:** 28
stone **4:** 4, 12, 26, 35, 39, 41
Stone Age **5:** 7
Stone Age ax **4:** 5
stoneware **4:** 22, 24, 25
strand **7:** 4, 20, 21, 28
stratosphere **9:** 20
straw **3:** 49
strength of metal alloys **2:** 23
strength of wood **3:** 24-26
strengthening glass **5:** 24-27
strengthening, strengthening agents in paper **3:** 48, 49, 54
stretching fibers **7:** 36
strontium carbonate **5:** 9
studding **3:** 38
styrene **1:** 10
styrene-butadiene rubber **1:** 42
styrofoam **1:** 4, 14, 33; **6:** 57
sublimation **8:** 16, 17
subtractive colors **6:** 4
suction pump **9:** 5, 6
sugarcane **3:** 49
suits of armor **2:** 43, 44
sulfur **1:** 13, 27, 29, 43
sulfur dioxide **9:** 19, 46-47
summerwood **3:** 14
super glue **1:** 40, 41; **6:** 54
superconductivity in metals **2:** 9
superconductors **4:** 8, 45
superheated water **8:** 20, 54
surface coating glass **5:** 22
surface coatings **7:** 45, 56; **6:** 4-40
surface tension **8:** 11, 14, 25-26, 28, 37
surfactants **8:** 29
suspensions **8:** 6
sweaters **7:** 27, 44

swords **2**: 36, 40, 41, 42, 43, 44
synthetic adhesives **3**: 43, 44; **6**: 43, 49-50
synthetic ceramics **4**: 48
synthetic dye industry **6**: 15
synthetic dyes **6**: 7, 10, 14, 15, 26; **7**: 38
synthetic fibers **1**: 7, 13, 48, 50; **3**: 50; **7**: 7, 12, 14, 18, 24, 31, 38
synthetic polymers **1**: 6, 7; **7**: 14
synthetic resins **3**: 43, 44
synthetic rubber **1**: 6, 7, 13, 42
synthetics **1**: 7

T

tableware **4**: 16, 24, 25
tangled **7**: 21
tannins **3**: 10
tarmacadam **4**: 41
tarnishing **2**: 10, 11; **5**: 23
teak **3**: 17, 19
Teflon® **1**: 10, 41; **4**: 44
tektites **5**: 7
tempering metals **2**: 23, 41
tempering, tempered glass **5**: 25, 26
temporarily hard water **8**: 55
tensile glass temperature **7**: 17
tensile strength **7**: 7
tension weakness in ceramics **4**: 8
terra cotta **4**: 31
Terylene® **1**: 50; **7**: 33, 42
tetrafluoroethylene **1**: 10
thermal capacity **8**: 34, 36. *See also* heat capacity
thermal properties of glass **5**: 18
thermals **9**: 9
thermistors **4**: 53
thermometers **5**: 12, 53
thermoplastic adhesives **6**: 50
thermoplastic fibers **7**: 44
thermoplastic resins **1**: 11
thermoplastics **1**: 10, 11, 12, 13, 15, 20, 24, 31, 35, 43
thermosets, thermosetting plastics **1**: 11, 12, 13, 20, 22, 23, 24, 43, 44, 46, 57; **6**: 50; **7**: 44
thermosphere **9**: 20
thread **7**: 4, 22, 44, 49
tie dyeing **6**: 19
tiles, ceramic tiles **4**: 10, 16, 17, 21, 23, 24, 25, 26, 31, 42
timber **3**: 4, 34, 36, 38, 39
tin **2**: 8, 10, 24, 25, 26, 30, 37, 38, 40
tin ore **2**: 38
tin oxide **4**: 53
tin plating **2**: 30; **8**: 54
tinting glass **5**: 21
tin-vanadium oxide **4**: 51
tire cord **7**: 37, 41, 44, 49
tires **1**: 8, 42, 51; **9**: 28, 29
titanium **2**: 22, 50, 51, 54
titanium dioxide **4**: 46
toilet tissue **3**: 54
top coat **6**: 28, 30, 31, 34
tortoiseshell **1**: 46
toughened glass **5**: 25
toxic fumes or smoke **1**: 14, 25
transistor **4**: 6, 45
transition metals **2**: 8; **4**: 51
translucent plastics **1**: 12, 13, 30, 53
transparency in materials **1**: 4, 12, 21, 24, 26, 28, 30, 33, 34, 37, 38, 40, 52; **4**: 20, 50, 53; **5**: 4, 6, 15, 19; **6**: 27, 37, 38, 55

tree rings. *See* growth rings
tree trunks **3**: 6, 11, 12, 13, 14, 15, 16, 23, 27, 32, 33
Trevira® **7**: 42
triacetate **7**: 36
Tricel® **1**: 47; **7**: 46
tritium **8**: 14
troposphere **9**: 19, 20
trusses **2**: 54, 55
tube glass **5**: 53
tube metal **2**: 19, 44
tumblers **5**: 48
tungsten **2**: 9, 21, 53
tungsten carbide **4**: 57
tunnel kilns **4**: 19, 25, 28, 30, 31
turpentine **6**: 37
tweeds **7**: 27
twenty-four-carat gold **2**: 26
twine **7**: 11, 22

U

unbleached paper **3**: 56
undercoat **6**: 28, 30, 31, 33
universal solvent **8**: 43
unreactive metals **2**: 4, 8, 11
uPVC. *See* polyvinyl chloride
uranium **5**: 11
uranium oxides **4**: 54
urea **1**: 44
urethane **1**: 53
utility poles **3**: 28

V

V. *See* vinyl and polyvinyl chloride
vacuum **9**: 6, 35, 55
vacuum forming **1**: 19, 20
vacuum pump **9**: 8, 11, 13
valency forces **6**: 45
valve **9**: 6, 7, 28, 31, 39
vapor **8**: 4. *See also* water vapor
vaporize, vaporization **8**: 16
varnishes **1**: 11; **6**: 37, 38
vat dyeing **6**: 20-21
veneers **3**: 9, 18, 42, 43; **6**: 42
Venetian glassmakers **5**: 36
vinyl (V) **1**: 26, 28, 34-38. *See also* polyvinyl chloride
vinyl acetate **1**: 39; **7**: 45
vinyl chloride **1**: 10; **7**: 45
vinyl emulsion **6**: 34
vinyl varnishes **6**: 37
vinyl wallpaper **6**: 47
viscose fiber **1**: 47, 50; **6**: 20; **7**: 36, 39, 40, 41
viscose process **7**: 36, 39-41
viscosity of gases **9**: 13, 15
viscosity of water **8**: 14, 32, 39
vitreous china **4**: 20
vitreous enamel, vitreous enameling **4**: 23; **5**: 13, 14; **5**: 13, 14
vitrify, vitrification **4**: 19-20, 22, 25, 27, 28

W

wallboards **4**: 34
wallpaper adhesive **6**: 47
warping **3**: 19, 24
wash and wear fabrics **7**: 44
waste paper **3**: 56, 57
water **7**: 7, 10, 17, 18; **9**: 4, 5, 16, 21, 22, 27, 30, 46, 47, 48, 53, 54; **8**: 4 AND THROUGHOUT
water-based adhesives **6**: 49, 55, 57

water-based paints **6**: 29, 34-35, 36
water cycle **8**: 4-6
water heaters **8**: 33, 38
water, influence on properties of wood **3**: 20-24, 28
water in papermaking **3**: 50-51
water molecules **8**: 8-13, 44
waterproof fibers **7**: 8, 18, 26, 48
waterproofing **8**: 28-29
waterproof or watertight ceramics **4**: 9, 10, 11, 19, 20, 21, 22, 23, 25, 29
water softeners **8**: 55
water vapor **8**: 4, 6, 16, 17, 19, 20, 49; **9**: 3, 9, 16, 19, 21, 36, 49, 51-53
Watt, James **2**: 56
waxes **3**: 10
wear resistance of metal alloys **2**: 23
weaving **7**: 7, 8, 22, 23
web of paper **3**: 51
welding **1**: 18, 22, 29, 37; **2**: 27, 52
wet felting **3**: 45
wet spinning **7**: 36, 40
wetting **6**: 46-47
wetting agents **8**: 28-29
wet water **8**: 37
white glass **5**: 11, 36
white glue **6**: 54
whitewares **4**: 16, 22-26, 29, 30, 33
windows and window glass 7, 10, 42, 46, 49, 52
windshields **5**: 21, 23, 26, 27, 54
winning **4**: 28
wire **2**: 19, 31, 53
wire-reinforced glass **5**: 26
woad **6**: 13; **1**: 22, 37, 44, 45; **2**: 12, 15, 36, 40, 44, 46, 47, 48, 55; **3**: 4 AND THROUGHOUT; **5**: 7
wood cells **3**: 10. *See also* cells
wood chips **7**: 12, 38
wooden tiles **3**: 8
wood products in building **3**: 5, 7, 8, 16, 23, 26, 28, 34, 44
wood pulp processing **7**: 31
wool **1**: 13, 39, 51; **3**: 51; **6**: 14, 17; **7**: 6, 10, 19, 21, 26, 43, 45
worsteds **7**: 27
wrought iron **2**: 40, 41, 44, 49, 55

X

xenon **9**: 18, 54, 56

Y

yarn **7**: 22, 25, 28
yew **3**: 16, 17
yttrium vanadate **4**: 52

Z

Zachariasen, W. H. **5**: 39
zinc **2**: 3, 6, 10, 11, 13, 16, 24, 25, 26, 27, 30, 31, 41
zinc coating or plating **2**: 3, 6, 11, 13, 30, 31
zinc oxide **4**: 56; **5**: 9
zircon **4**: 52
zirconia **4**: 4, 53
zirconium dioxide. *See* zirconia
zirconium oxide **5**: 9
zirconium silicate. *See* zircon
zirconium–vanadium oxide **4**: 51